dancing
bones

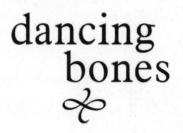

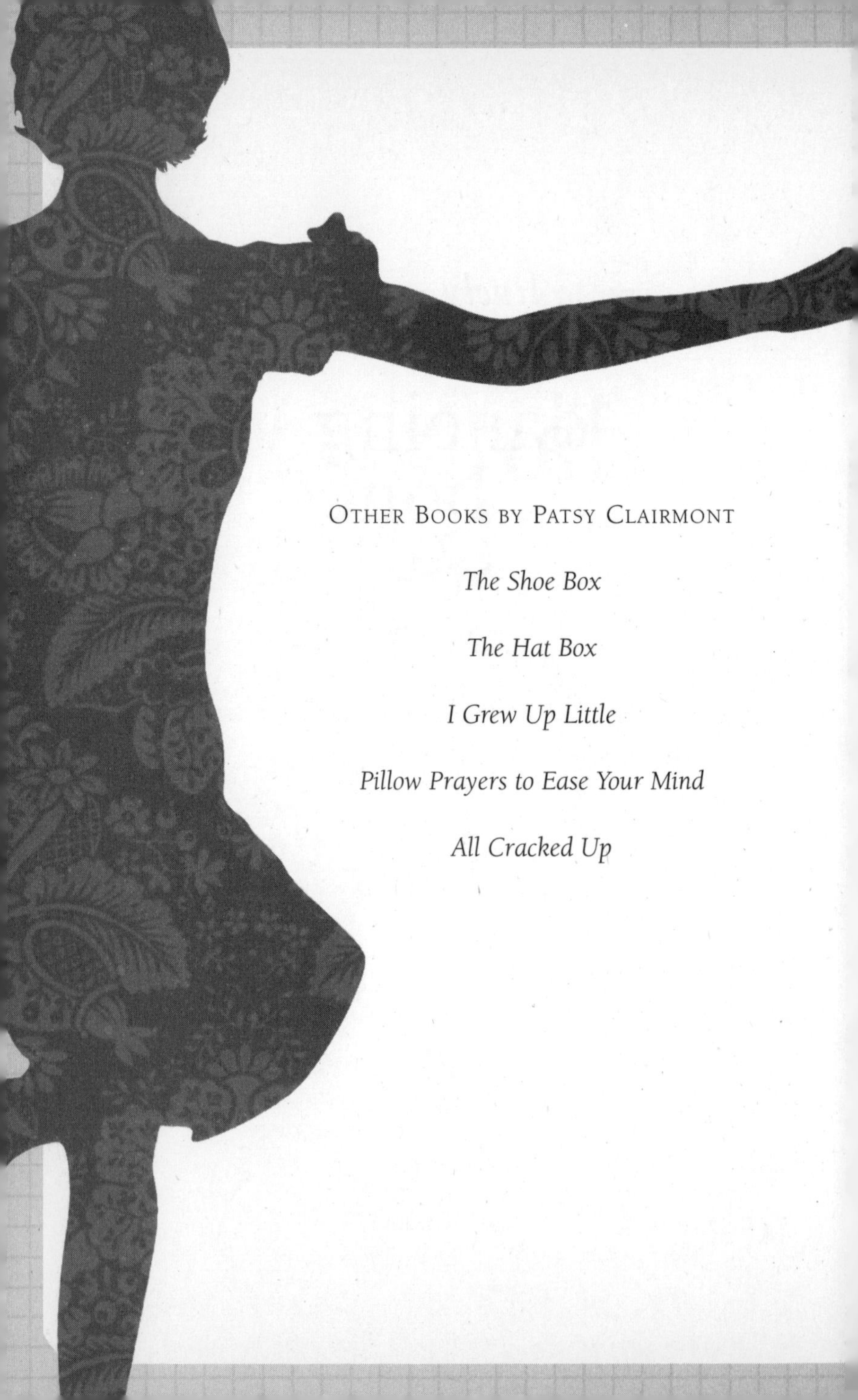

Other Books by Patsy Clairmont

The Shoe Box

The Hat Box

I Grew Up Little

Pillow Prayers to Ease Your Mind

All Cracked Up

LIVING *lively* IN THE VALLEY

dancing
bones

PATSY CLAIRMONT

Published by

THOMAS NELSON
Since 1798

www.thomasnelson.com

DANCING BONES

Copyright © 2007 Patsy Clairmont

All rights reserved. No portion of this book may be reproduced, stored in a retrieval
system, or transmitted in any form or by any means—electronic, mechanical, photocopy,
recording, or any other—except for brief quotations in printed reviews, without the
prior written permission of the publisher.

Published in Nashville by Thomas Nelson, Inc.

Thomas Nelson, Inc. books may be purchased in bulk for educational, business,
fund-raising, or sales promotional use. For information, please e-mail
SpecialMarkets@ThomasNelson.com.

All Scripture quotations, unless otherwise indicated, are taken from The New King James
Version (NKJV), copyright © 1979, 1980, 1982, Thomas Nelson, Inc., Publishers.

Other Scripture references are from the following sources:

The Holy Bible, New International Version (NIV). Copyright © 1973, 1978, 1984.
International Bible Society. Used by permission of Zondervan.

The Message (MSG), copyright © 1993. Used by permission of NavPress Publishing Group.

Library of Congress Cataloging-in-Publication Data

Clairmont, Patsy.
    Dancing bones : living lively in the valley / by Patsy Clairmont.
       p. cm.
    Includes bibliographical references and index.
    ISBN 13: 978-0-8499-0176-8 (hard cover)
    ISBN 10: 0-8499-0176-6 (hard cover)
    1. Christian women—Religious life. 2. Suffering—Religious aspects--Christianity.
I. Title.
BV4527.C5328 2007
248.8'43—dc22

                                          2006101037

Printed in the United States of America

07 08 09 10 11 12 QW 9 8 7 6 5 4 3

To Florence Littauer
who taught me early on in my ministry,
in a hundred different ways, to keep dancing.

contents

contents

*t*he hand of the LORD came upon me and brought me out in the Spirit of the LORD, and set me down in the midst of the valley; and it was full of bones. Then He caused me to pass by them all around, and behold, there were very many in the open valley; and indeed they were very dry. And He said to me, "Son of man, can these bones live?"

So I answered, "O Lord GOD, You know."

Again He said to me, "Prophesy to these bones, and say to them, 'O dry bones, hear the word of the LORD! Thus says the Lord GOD to these bones: "Surely I will cause breath to enter into you, and you shall live. I will put sinews on you and bring flesh upon you, cover you with skin and put breath in you; and you shall live. Then you shall know that I am the LORD."'"

So I prophesied as I was commanded; and as I prophesied, there was a noise, and suddenly a rattling; and the bones came together, bone to bone. Indeed, as I looked, the sinews and the flesh came upon them, and the skin covered them over; but there was no breath in them.

Also He said to me, "Prophesy to the breath, prophesy, son of man, and say to the breath, 'Thus says the Lord GOD: "Come from the four winds, O breath, and breathe on these slain, that they may live."'" So I prophesied as He commanded me, and breath came into them, and they lived, and stood upon their feet, an exceedingly great army.

EZEKIEL 37:1–10

one

COME DANCE WITH ME

*a*s a teen, I spent more Friday nights than I can count at my best friend's house. Carol and I would dance away the hours until we would drop our weary bones in a heap on the floor. As soon as we could catch our breath, we would get up, giggle, and start in again. Nothing took us to the mountaintop of our teenage emotions like rocking around the clock.

Carol's huge, cedar-paneled upstairs bedroom was perfect for trying out all the latest dance steps: the stroll, the chicken, and the twist. We would bebop until Carol's mom would holler up the steps that the chandeliers were swinging and chunks of plaster were ricocheting off the living room ceiling.

Now, forty-five-plus years later, we're still dancing. While Carol remains a dancing machine, I'm more likely to sway than to do the pony. Break dancing sounds more like a threat than an invitation.

Speaking of dancing, have you ever read Ezekiel 37? It talks about a whole valley full of folks who'd lost their rhythm. It seems these people had the dance knocked out of them until they crumbled into a heap of bones on the valley floor. Sound familiar? Sound like last Tuesday? It does for me. In fact, it's probably something we can all relate to. That's why I think it's worth spending a little time looking at that valley in Ezekiel—and our own valleys.

But first, let me welcome you, girlfriend, to the valley experience. You've probably been here before. This is where you've met Reality. You know her, the one with the piercing megaphone voice; beehive hairdo; polyester pants; polka-dotted, horn-rimmed spectacles (Reality *is* a spectacle); combat boots; and backpack full of survival pamphlets.

Truth be known, most of us wish Reality looked more like Gwyneth Paltrow or Julia Roberts. Who invited Miss Party-Pooper? I'd rather have someone who could inspire me to skip to the summit of life. On the big screen, Gwyneth almost always achieves her dreams. But no, we get Raunchy Reality, insisting we hunker down in the valley, of all places, and make ourselves at home.

Still pining for the mountains? You're not alone.

I was on a cross-country flight recently when my plane flew over a range of snowy summits. My eyes traced the roadways up the rocky sides to see if any of the trails would take a car to the top. None of them did. Isn't that just like life? It's never quite that easy to get to the top. I've watched on television as climbers, on arriving at the pinnacle, splay out their arms and do a high step to celebrate their achievement. Why? They're probably delirious from the effort. But beyond their temporary euphoria, I have to wonder if there's not a part of them deep down that thinks if they can just get to the top, they'll escape all the hassles and hardships of the valley.

Behind all that mountain hoopla, we seem to think we can shake off the valley dust of routine and hardships. And maybe even get closer to God. In the Bible, the mountaintop often signifies the place where God speaks, as with Moses on Mount Sinai or the disciples on the Mount of Transfiguration. So maybe we shimmy up the rocky cliffs in hopes of having our own transforming experience.

Some people climb for the view. Our perspective changes when we're on top. Before our eyes are spread distant shores, valley dips, roadways, and riverbeds like ribbons curling on the package of the land. Yes, mountaintops lend themselves to grandeur and greatness.

But here is the breath-stopping truth: we are called to live the majority of our lives in the valley. Uh-huh, most of our days are spent in the earth's indentions. Now where's the music in that? Who volunteers to don a kilt and do the Highland fling to that news?

That would be me. Yup, I'm jazzed about valley living (well, most of the time), and let me tell you why. From the mountaintop I can see an eagle soar, but I've learned that in the valley I can hear a sparrow sing. On the mountain I see trees like canopies, but in the valley I can sit in their shade and eat of their fruit. On the mountain I see lakes like small mirrors, but in the valley I can touch the reflections and ladle the water to my parched lips. On the summit I see people like walking sticks, but in the valley I can trace a child's face and dab away tears.

So sit down with me and Ms. Reality, and listen up. Or, better yet, put on your dancin' shoes and join us. Eventually, we'll learn that the mountaintop is distant and dangerous. But in the meantime, let's see how the valley is fruitful and dangerous. Because life is like that: bone-drying hard and wildly wondrous.

Jesus Christ knew that. He came from the high places but lived out his thirty-three years among us in the valley.

He began his human life in a lowly manger and completed his work on a barren hillside that became divinely lush with his holy sacrifice. Hope spilled out of his pierced side and into the valley. In that valley, birds sang inspired arias, leaves pirouetted to the earth with elegance, and breezes carried the grace melody throughout the lowlands. You still can hear the music in a bee's buzz, smell it in the lilacs' sweetness, and see it in a snowflake's dance. Listen carefully. . . . There, did you hear it? If you didn't, you will.

We Valley Girls have a reason to tap our toes and move our feet. We won't always hear the music, but even during those dark times, we can keep dancing by faith.

In the pages ahead, we'll meet women who have done that very thing. They will teach us some new steps to help us develop a broader repertoire. And we'll hear a spectrum of thought on what it means to survive—and thrive—in the everyday muddle of our fast-paced existence. They will remind us that we're not alone in our quest to dance in the valley.

Dancing Bones is designed with you in mind. I know life isn't easy for you, because I've spoken with tens of thousands of you in my travels with Women of Faith over the past eleven years. I've been stunned at your losses and the difficulties you function with daily. I'm aware you live in the valley with only occasional visits to the mountaintop for a breath of unsullied air. I offer you a fresh perspective to help you maintain and, if necessary, resuscitate your verve.

Valleys are rich with life and littered with liabilities, which means we'll have to step lively, and periodically we'll visit the mountaintop to maintain perspective.

Hang on to your spandex as we tour together the valley to see what the well-dressed Valley Girl is wearing these days, to examine the cost to maintain not only our wardrobes but also our sanity. We will laugh, think, twirl, and sip the latest caramel frappé concoction, as we chat about current events in our lives.

So dig out some comfy shoes, dust off your dry bones, and get ready to dance!

two

VALLEY PICNIC:
WITH ANTS, OF COURSE

*l*ife ain't no picnic!" How many times have you heard Ms. Reality Check spout that one? If I have to hear one more time, "No pain, no gain," I think I'll karate-chop the messenger. Or how about, "If life gives you lemons, make lemonade?" I pucker at the thought.

Yes, yes, we've all been told that the "school of hard knocks" is part of life, but if you're like me, crushing blows still catch you off guard, leave you speechless, and at times rob you of your very breath.

I really do believe that in this life we will have scrumptious picnic spreads of fried chicken, corn on the cob, and homemade ice cream. But not without ants, mosquitoes, and nasty sunburns.

Some friends of mine live in a country setting, and they love to eat outside next to their pool. Their teenage daughter, after enjoying one of their family picnics, began to itch and then broke out in red-peppered spots. Turns out she had developed such sensitivity to poison ivy that just being around the plant, crossing its fumes, caused her body to react. She was in distress for days.

As long as I understand that the valley, where bees nest and poison ivy spreads, is where I'll usually be eating the contents of my packed basket, I can safeguard my heart from disillusionment. I understand that I won't be spending lots of time sipping sweet nectar on a distant mountaintop.

We do visit mountaintops every once in a while, but the majority of our sojourn is in the valley. Ask the disciples Peter, John, and James, who after "picnicking" with Jesus, Moses, and Elijah on the Mount of Transfiguration wanted to pitch tents and stay there forever. Who wouldn't? Why, they were in the afterglow of a miracle. Besides, the view was divine and the company heavenly, so why would anyone choose to leave? Yet Jesus led his disciples back down into the valley to finish their work amid insults, treachery, and death.

Why? Love. Love motivated Jesus to endure all that was before him in his valley, it motivated his disciples, and his love will keep us even in the midst of our thicket-ridden experiences.

When Ms. Reality Check comes rapping at my heart's door, I find her too blunt. ("Yes, that does make your butt look big!") What she says is hard to bear because often we've had such high expectations for our daily existence, fueled by society's hedonistic mentality that tells us we should be multitasking, svelte, career-oriented, fun-seeking women.

Ms. Reality Check, while appearing to be a wet blanket at our picnic, is offering us truth. But it might do her—and us—well if she would dip her insights into mercy's pool before wrapping us up in them.

Truth can be brutal, which, I'm sure, is why some counseling takes years before an individual grows strong enough and courageous enough to face her interior wounds without further splintering.

Now, some may object and counter with, "I knew all along life wouldn't be perfect, but I thought it would be easier than what I'm going through." I can identify with that. We are told repeatedly in Scripture to prepare for hardships; so why do we believe our lives should be char- acterized by ease? Do you think it may be the hope of heaven within us that makes us willing to risk expecting the best? Or is it fantasy? Or denial? My best guess is that we flutter about like a butterfly to the flowers of hope, fantasy, and denial, depending on the situation and our ability to bear it.

Hope is a buoy to help keep our heads above the waterline of reality. Yet, when we depend on it to be our protection against difficulties, we deflate hope, and it becomes a weighted sinker that drags down our faith. Hope doesn't announce that life is safe, therefore, we will be; instead, it whispers that Christ is our safety in the midst of harsh reality.

That's the good news about picnics in the valley. We don't want to miss the views while we mindlessly shuffle our feet, waiting for mountains to rise up under us. Instead, we want to spread a gingham cloth in a valley of clover and picnic on the Lord's kind mercies in the midst of heartbreak and disappointment. In the shade of his presence, we experience Christ's tender care for our bruised emotions.

Our view from the valley *is* different from the mountain view, and it's invaluable. Mountaintop views are breathtaking, while valley views are life-giving. If we experience a church only from the tip of its steeple, we miss the heart of the place, its altar. We are children of the lowlands who walk through a dangerous world filled with enemies and riches untold. But we can be heartened in the lowlands, knowing it is where the majority of the fruit grows. We fruit-bearers were meant to share the bounty with other valley inhabitants. And what's a picnic without fresh fruit? (Pass the strawberry shortcake, please.)

VALLEY VIEW

When was the last time you went on a picnic? Last week? Last year? Or perhaps it's been so long you can't remember. Well, don't put it off a moment longer. Pick up a few goodies, pull out a basket, and get ready for some fun! You say the weather doesn't allow it? Okay, spread a cloth on the family room floor and see life and lunch from a new view.

When weather and time permit, attend your picnic via bicycle. By the time you arrive, the aromas emitting from your lunch will stimulate your saliva glands. If you don't have a basket on your bike, a backpack might do the trick.

You could motor to a mountaintop, but I suggest a fertile valley, even if it's your backyard vegetable garden. What could compare to a vine-ripened tomato or a freshly pulled carrot? Give it a healthy squirt under a hose, and you're good to go.

In your basket include a mini-loaf of French bread, a soft spread (my favorite is cashew butter), a clump of frozen grapes, and a chilled bottle of water. Or you can go full throttle and take a gourmet offering. But a picnic menu doesn't have to be complicated.

In fact, part of the joy of food outside is imbibing in the simple pleasures of life, such as slurping chilled watermelon while being serenaded by the brown thrasher on yonder limb. Just make sure you're not sitting under the feathered songster, lest some of the notes she hits cause an unseemly splash.

You might want to bring a friend, a journal, and a New Testament. Jot down inspirations and ponder valley life and the Shepherd who walks with us there. A meaningful conversation makes a meal a memory.

We may live in the valley, but we can find myriad ways to make mealtime divine. Bon appetit!

three

VALLEY BONES: FROM ONE
FEMUR TO ANOTHER

*W*hen transported by God's hand to a valley, Ezekiel had no idea what awaited him. The sight before him made it clear this was no picnic. Valleys usually offer a variety of places to spread a cloth and unload a basket of food, but this location already was full—full of bones. Even if Ezekiel had found a shade tree to eat under, one tends to lose one's appetite in the presence of a corpse, much less a whole valley full of disjointed folks.

After Ezekiel viewed the valley full of bones, God asked Ezekiel an odd question: "Can these bones live?"

Huh? Dry bone on top of crispy dry bone? I mean,

what're the chances? Why, I've looked at people who were alive and wondered if they would make it; so I know I would have failed the bone-test question.

Speaking of bone tests, I failed mine. Seems that as the years careened by, they did so right over the top of my bones. The flipping of the calendar pages didn't crush my bones; it just sucked out all the suppleness, leaving them brittle. Now I'm a delicate porcelain doll. Okay, okay, maybe not a doll, more like a fragile cracked pot—a term that has defined me most of my life, dry bones or not.

But Ezekiel didn't guess at God's plan or deny God's power. He answered the question simpl: "O, Lord GOD, You know."

Wow. I wish I could grab hold of the truth in that answer for my life so that when trials come, I don't immediately assume all is gloom and doom. Instead, I could rest assured that God knows what he is doing, even if it looks like a hopeless, lifeless situation to me.

The part of this account that I like best is when God has

Ezekiel prophesy to the bones that they will come back to life—and there is a "rattling." Rattling bones either sound spooky or life-giving, depending on your perspective.

Erring on the side of fear, I spent a lot of spooked years as an agoraphobic. Had I been present at Ezekiel's healing service during that season of my life, I would have run and hid in my cave on hearing the rattling bones and missed the dance of life as the bones came together. How sad for me.

Today I like to think of the resurrection rattling as valley music, a sound worthy of a grand picnic. Although I admit that in the mornings my bones do more popping than rattling as I attempt a resurrection out of my bed and then weave toward the kitchen, opening curtains and shades along the way. It takes an inner pep talk to get these old, porous bones up and dancing through the day. I've wondered if WD-40 might be a good lubricant to keep handy in my bathrobe pocket. When my bones were reluctant to go forth, I'd just give them a couple of generous squirts and they'd loosen right up. Then I could boogie into my schedule.

Actually, what I've found most helpful in keeping the rhythm of life oozing within me is the same thing Ezekiel used in his valley of bones to rouse such a great army: "O, dry bones, hear the word of the LORD!"

VALLEY VIEW

If life has dried up your enthusiasm, if your faith feels brittle, or if valley life has left you parched, I encourage you to delve into the life-giving, bone-lubricating truths of Scripture. In fact, let's begin with my favorite psalm, which I memorized as a child. Beware, it has a snappy tempo that could cause your toe to tap, and a desire may well up within you to pack a picnic basket and skip to a park.

> Make a joyful shout to the LORD, all you lands!
> Serve the LORD with gladness;
> Come before His presence with singing.
> Know that the LORD, He is God;
> It is He who has made us, and not we ourselves;
> We are His people and the sheep of His pasture.
> Enter into His gates with thanksgiving,
> And into His courts with praise.
> Be thankful to Him, and bless His name.
> For the LORD is good;
> His mercy is everlasting,
> And His truth endures to all generations.
>
> PSALM 100

Valley Bones: From one femur to another

Write out this WD-40 psalm and tape it to your morning mirror. Read it daily until it sings within your bones. I promise that, when you twirl about in gladness and high-step your way into joy, even your valleys will have picnic potential.

four

VALLEY LIGHT:
DAZZLING MOMENTS

I said to the man who stood at the gate of the year, "Give me a light
that I might tread safely into the unknown." And he replied, "Go out
into the darkness and put your hand into the hand of God. That
shall be to you better than light and safer than a known way!"
—MINNIE LOUISE HASKINS

Our six-year-old grandson, Justin, stared down at his opened birthday present uncertain what he was looking at. His poppa thought a youngster would have great fun navigating the dark by donning a headlamp such as miners wear. Once Justin understood the lamp, he looked pleased with the prospect of lighting up otherwise scary places.

He's not the only one. Regardless of our age, nothing is more welcome in darkness than light. Even a lit match in a dark place brings a sigh of relief. A speck of light is revealing; it gives us a place to head for, and it offers hope. Perhaps that's why fireworks are so popular. They create, even if just for a moment, light over our shadowed world.

On a recent trip to Israel, I stayed in a ninth-floor Tel Aviv hotel room overlooking the Mediterranean Sea. On the second evening of our stay, the tour group was surprised and delighted to find out that France was bringing in a boatload of fireworks that they would shoot off over the water as a gift to Israel. The festivities would take place across the street from our hotel, which gave us a ringside seat to the dancing light across the sky.

The people of Tel Aviv lined up on the beach, in parking lots, and in the streets. Literally thousands of them flooded in to view the spectacle. They came on foot, in cars, on motorcycles, and in buses. My roommate, Jan, and I watched from our balcony as the people gathered, and then the heavens lit up with explosive flashes of light.

After the impressive show was over, a secondary light show began as the viewers tried to make their way home. Jan and I had never witnessed such a long snarl of traffic, and because our room was on a high floor, we could see taillights for miles in all directions. Four hours later the cars were still bumper to bumper, trying to inch away. The following morning the newspaper proclaimed it the worst traffic jam in the city's history.

All to see streaks of speckled light dance in the night air.

While on our trip in Israel, we toured the Holocaust museum, Yad Vashem, which was a beautifully designed display of tragedy. Your heart breaks to think other human hearts could be so dark as to commit such atrocities. The Children's section, which is in a separate building, has a cavelike entrance that leads you into a darkened space where pinpoints of reflected light surround you. Each dot of light represents one of the 1.5 million children who were killed. Overhead you hear a voice read each child's name, age, and country. The experience was wrenching, and yet the tiny dots of light held such beauty on the velvet backdrop of pain. It was a stunning way to remember those innocent victims.

In the beginning God brought physical light into our dark world and then separated the darkness and the light, and he called the light "morning" and the darkness "evening." On the fourth day he made the light holders: the sun, the moon, and the stars. Eventually, God sent his Son, Jesus, into the world to be the Light Bearer, that he might expose and illuminate the darkness of our own hearts as well as the evil that hovers in our land. Jesus came to redeem us in the midst of darkness and chaos that we might become "children of the day," that we might be light holders. As children of the light, we partner with Christ to bring illumination to those around us, that we might offer them the hope he has given us.

The day before we left Jerusalem, I watched my friend Mary cup her hands around her eyes so she could peek through a window into a tiny store. "I think if this store were open, I'd find everything I've been looking for to take back to the States."

Jan and I joined her at the window and peered through the glass, agreeing that the shop looked intriguing. So we made plans to return the following day.

When we entered the shop the next morning, we were smitten with the lovely items that filled the cases and shelves—not to mention the gentle watercolors that crowded the walls. The owner was a winsome Irish woman named Claire who was married to the artist of those inspiring paintings. Claire immediately won our hearts with her sweet charm.

As we browsed, Claire told us that she had a friend visiting from England, Stefan, whom she hadn't seen for twenty-seven years. Then she told us that he had inoperable cancer and they were uncertain how long he had left to live. Claire obviously was feeling jolted by her friend's illness.

A short time later, as we continued to investigate the paintings and handmade jewelry, Stefan entered the store. He was a dear man with lively eyes and a quick wit. After exchanging pleasantries, he asked me what type of work we did. I told him about Women of Faith and the thousands of women we meet with every week to encourage in their life's journey.

Then I asked Stefan what he did. "I work for a publisher. I'm not a person of faith; in fact, I'm an atheist."

My heart sank to think that this man was dying but had no faith to show him the higher path or to comfort his heart in scary hours. I knew his life and mine would touch only for a moment and then I would never see him again, so I prayed that God would make my words candles to help Stefan consider a bright future in his darkest hours.

Stefan mentioned his cancer, so I asked gently, "How do you handle your terminal diagnosis without faith? I so rely on mine to help me during bleak times."

He responded, "I try not to think about my illness or it becomes too much."

"That must be a full-time effort, pushing back the reality of your situation."

Then Stefan announced, "This is my third bout with cancer. I had it in my twenties, then again later when they removed my right ear. But now they say they can't do anything for me." He paused. "Actually, I feel blessed."

Surprised by Stefan's choice of words, as if a match had been lit, I asked, "Stefan, as an atheist, who blesses you?"

He gazed off for a moment as he considered the question. "Well, I guess that would be God."

"Oh, Stefan," I replied, "I think you have more space for God inside you than you know."

"Well, it's strange that you would say that, because yesterday I went to the Wailing Wall, and I prayed. I prayed." He seemed surprised by his own actions. "Why, that's the first time I've offered up a prayer to God since my bar mitzvah as a young boy."

"Oh, yes, you definitely have more room in your heart for God than you may have considered, Stefan."

Mary and Jan had paid for their treasures and were ready to leave the shop. I so wanted to pray for my new friend, but I knew it was risky to ask. I didn't want to offend him. Still, I didn't want to leave without at least asking.

"Stefan, would it make you uncomfortable or offend you if I prayed for you aloud right now?"

He studied me for a moment. "I would welcome it."

So I prayed, not an especially articulate prayer, but a sincere one. When I finished, the little store seemed awash in the candlelight of God's love.

My heart was full of gratitude for those shared moments. Our conversation was probably no more than fifteen minutes, but I suspected God had Stefan on a revelation path, a defining path of new beginnings. I felt as though God had allowed me to hold up a candle along Stefan's way. I didn't sense I had changed Stefan's mind, but instead that God was gently at work in this dear man's heart.

"Stefan, I shall not forget you, and I will keep you in my prayers," I promised.

"And I shall not forget you," he answered.

An atheistic Jew and a Christian cracked pot—only God could have had our paths cross. Stefan was visiting Israel from England, and I was visiting from America. And even though I don't know what happened inside Stefan's heart, it felt to me as if God was doing something significant in the closing chapter of his life.

VALLEY VIEW

In the Psalms, David says, "Your word is a lamp to my feet and a light to my path" (119:105).

His Word becomes our headlamp, showing us the next step to take and reminding us that we aren't alone, even in the valley of the shadow of death.

Take a moment to imagine what a difference one small candle makes in a dark room. In fact, sit in a dark room for several reflective moments and then carefully light a candle and see the impact it makes. It is a strong reminder of what we can be while living in this dark world.

Valley Friends

Betty Jo Morgan's grandson Connor Phillips was diagnosed with cancer when he was just two years old, but chemotherapy knocked out the disease, and Connor was launched into a happy childhood as a healthy, rambunctious, ornery little Texas boy. All went well until a couple of years ago, when Connor's dad died of cancer about the same time Connor's cancer returned. An osteosarcoma tumor had wrapped itself around nine-year-old Connor's jugular vein, and the surgery to remove it took eighteen hours.

As Connor recovered, his family wanted to give him something to keep him busy and take his mind off his problems. The Morgans live in East Texas, and the family has a long-standing tradition for the youngsters to show hogs with their 4-H club at the county fair. So Connor was given a hog to tend to and groom, and when the fair rolled around, he entered his hog in the competition.

It didn't win a thing.

But that's not the end of the story. Although Connor's hog didn't win a prize, it *was* selected for the fair's auction. So there he stood in the ring, a little boy with his hog, and the bidding started.

You know, an auction isn't a price-tag sale. It's an event that requires bids from more than one prospective buyer. In this case the auction was a *community* gesture. Those friends, neighbors, and business owners from Connor's community, recognizing an opportunity to lift a courageous little guy (and his family) out of the valley, kept bidding and bidding and bidding until the winning bidder walked away with an imperfect hog, and Connor walked away with $36,000, the most ever paid in the history of the Montgomery County Fair livestock auction.

At the Women of Faith conference in Houston, Betty Jo told us her grandson is "still an ornery little guy," but she said it with pride and laughter in her voice. And some pain as well. You see, doctors had just found another tumor in Connor's neck. So his family doesn't know what the future holds for this tough little boy. But at the fair they found confirmation that they live in a grand-champion community of friends and neighbors ready to extend a hand and hold up a candle in the midst of Connor's shadowy valley. Whatever is ahead, they take the next step bravely holding God's hand.

five

VALLEY FOG: HAZY DAYS

*f*og hung in the New Mexico night sky like ancient draperies closing off visibility. Our plane circled and then began its descent through the thick folds of fabric to the runway below. But we passengers were jarred as the pilot pulled the plane's nose sharply up and headed back toward the shrouded stars.

After circling several more times, the pilot announced over the intercom that he was going to "try" to land again. Now, call me finicky, but "try" sounded way too unconfident. I wanted more assurance—like certifiable proof of pilot training, character references from his mother, and the results of his last sobriety test.

The pilot explained that the fog had created a heavy barrier, preventing him from seeing the runway, even feet away from touchdown. He laughed as he reported our predicament. Somehow, I didn't catch the humor. From what I could tell, as I scanned the other passengers' faces, the pilot seemed to be the only one having a missed-the-runway chuckle. Every fog-related accident I had ever seen on a television flash-danced through my mind.

On the next attempt we made it, but as soon as our wheels touched down, the airport closed the runway until dawn, when the sun would help burn off the soupy weather.

To think, all that drama over something as elemental as air!

Recently, as I perused a book of Western art, I came across an oil painting of a man looking over a fog-cloaked lake. In the distance looms a faint indication of mountains. The man's back faces the viewer, so you aren't distracted by what he looks like, yet you're aware of his solitary presence etched against this mysterious setting. The foggy drama unfolding in front of him adds a shiver of loneliness and a cloak of secrecy.

I had a feeling the setting for the painting was a coastal cove in Scotland at sunset. But it could just as well have been a place in the painter's mind that depicted his personal struggle with life's hidden intricacies.

We've all felt the fog of confusion, when we couldn't figure out life's whys, when we have stood on the banks of our life-scape gazing into the mist. Dense fog also encompasses us when we're depressed, making it difficult to slough through a day. Then there's the creeping fog that makes its way over our minds as we grow older.

My mind isn't nearly as snappy as it was when I was in my forties. Even my vocabulary plays hide-and-seek with my brain. My desire to learn has increased, but my ability to retain is similar to a partially clogged sieve. I'll hear something profound and think to myself, *I'll never forget that.* Hours later I'll remember that I wanted to remember something, but I have no idea what it was.

Why, even information I've known for years seems at times covered in a drift of gray air. I need a defogger for my head . . . hmm, I wonder who installs those. I mean, really, if we can inflate bosoms like hot air balloons and pooch up lips into voluptuous kissers, why not a brain defogger?

I must say, blips in my brain don't enhance my personality either. I get agitated with myself and then come off snippy. Yes, yes, snippy. I confess.

Sometimes I laugh at myself and with my friends as

their brains and mine skip a beat, but I think we all feel a little scared that it might be something more serious than a foggy moment. We wonder, *What if this never lifts and I lose my way? What if I forget my way home?*

My mother had Alzheimer's—an insidious, brain-consuming fog—so I've witnessed what happens to those who leave us one memory at a time. No one would volunteer for that tour of duty. I must say, some memories would be a relief to forget, but none of us wants to have our memory bank ever so slowly, yet permanently, erased.

During a break at a Women of Faith conference, a pleasant-looking woman approached me and asked me to sign her book. As I did, she told me that she had Alzheimer's and that she had come to the conference escorted by friends and family. She said, "I can do some pretty ridiculous things, but so far we've mostly learned to laugh together over them."

I've read that valley fog can be up to fifteen hundred feet thick, and I realized that was what that woman would be facing first mentally and then physically. I so admired her attitude and courage. She seemed to have the blessed gift of peace that comes with relinquishment to God's greater plan.

I'm not suggesting Alzheimer's is a great plan, because it's not—it's brutal and merciless. But I am suggesting that if we can rest in the confidence that no matter what fog-bank we end up in, God will care for us, in time liberate us from it, and use our tragedies for higher purposes than we could ever imagine—that is a greater plan. A plan of provision, of liberation, of redemption.

We're aware that at the fall of man disease became part of the norm, but when we're the recipients of a staggering diagnosis, we can't help but cry out, "Why?"

I don't know why we think knowing that answer would help to end our struggle. Even if we knew, we still would object vehemently. Sometimes I think my whys are nothing more than my ranting because life isn't the way I want it to be.

I'm a romantic at heart. I like fairy tales. I enjoy "and they lived happily ever after." At times I would have liked to step into the pages of a novel or a TV program and lived in that setting—maybe Mitford, Green Gables, Bedford, or Mayberry. Not that all went well in those made-up places, but problems always seemed to work themselves out so that they fit more comfortably into a heart (and an hour).

On *The Andy Griffith Show*, the character Barney Fife entangled himself in plenty of messes in Mayberry, but somehow the lovable deputy never stayed stuck long. How entertaining it would be to have him living nearby. And how delightful to think of Andy Taylor as one's next-door neighbor and local sheriff, handling nothing scarier than the latest spoiled child or speeding bicyclist (yeah—that would be me). I'd love to have Aunt Bee toting casseroles to our front door or to hire young Opie to mow the grass. I want the fog cleared away so I can see that in my future.

But the truth is Barney (Don Knotts) died at the age of eighty-one; Andy (Andy Griffith) is now in his eighties; Aunt Bee (Frances Bavier) passed away in 1989 at the age of eighty-seven; and Opie (Ron Howard) is now over fifty, and I hear he no longer needs the pocket change from cutting grass. And what about Mayberry? Well, I couldn't find a route to get us there, not even with MapQuest.

That kind of startling information blows the fog away from "pretend" in a hurry. (Of course, I could have checked my driver's license if I truly wanted an abrupt update.) It also reminds us that sometimes the fog that hides the future protects us from fretting over difficulties to come— difficulties that we're not ready to face. During our valley tenure, some events will pierce our hearts like sharp sticks that can't be dislodged. I'm comforted to know that, in God's sovereign hand and perfect timing, my worst dilemmas will be redeemed for good.

I used to believe that we would see the redemption of

all personal disasters resolved in our lifetime. That if we waited long enough, prayed hard enough, stood firm enough, we would see the results of our labor and faith. In some instances that's true, for God is tenderhearted toward us. But now I've lived long enough and experienced enough heartache and loss to realize that I'll die before I see all the answers I've prayed for. I'll pass away with a buildup of residual pain still in me because I've walked through the valley trenches. I believe that our Redeemer will perform his good pleasure on his own time card, which means that very likely some—if not many—of my concerns will be resolved after my departure.

My friend and coworker Sheila Walsh gave me the children's book *The Miraculous Journey of Edward Tulane*. Inside the cover an epigraph reads, "The heart breaks and breaks and lives by breaking. . . ." As I pondered that line, I realized that if our hearts didn't break, they would burst from pain and we would die. I never thought about heartbreaks helping us to survive this fractured world we live in, and yet they do.

When my dear friend Carol buried her adult son, Jeff, I wondered if her splintered heart would ever heal. I've watched her walk through twelve years since her loss, and I realize that while today Carol's life isn't paralyzed by Jeff's death, she still walks with a heart-limp, for as long as she's wearing her valley shoes, there is nowhere she can go to escape the reality of her loss.

Yet what I've witnessed, as my shy friend steps through the fog of despair and wrenching loss, is a growing boldness, a wider faith, a deeper compassion, a fearlessness toward death, and a heightened commitment toward her family.

It took time for Carol's dance to return, because it's hard to move your feet through the fog of loss, depression, and anger; but now she actually glides with greater grace than before. Her movements have an added lilt and precision. And others watch . . . and marvel . . . and wonder . . . and hope—hope that their own dance will return as well.

Valley View

I wonder, if the disciple Peter hadn't peered through the fog of fear, would he have walked around on the water with Jesus, enjoying the waves instead of sinking in his insecurities? Perhaps, if Peter's vision had been clear of fear after Christ was arrested, he would have defended Christ instead of denying him. What do you think?

What fogs your vision? Insecurities? Fears? List them.

Isn't it interesting that our fears and insecurities overlap and feed each other? Use the lists you've composed to create a new prayer emphasis in your life.

I've done many studies on what Scripture has to say about fear, which have been invaluable to me in scary moments. Try looking up the word *fear* in a concordance and then follow that ribbon of thought through the Bible. You'll discover many folks were in a fog, hampered by their fright. Memorizing the verses that dance off the page and resonate in my soul also helps me. Here are a few:

"There is no fear in love; but perfect love casts out fear, because fear involves torment" (1 John 4:18).

"For God has not given us a spirit of fear, but of power and of love and of a sound mind" (2 Timothy 1:7).

"The LORD is my light and my salvation; whom shall I fear? The LORD is the strength of my life; of whom shall I be afraid?" (Psalm 27:1).

VALLEY FRIENDS

Monica Darr was so dismayed when she found a lump in her breast she couldn't even step out of the fog of her fear and bring herself to go to the doctor. Instead, Larry, her devoted husband of twenty-five years, went for her. As a self-employed couple with no insurance and three kids in college, the Darrs knew they were in for a rough ride financially just to learn what the lump was, let alone to treat it, if it turned out to be cancerous.

Her husband looked around for help and was fortunate to find Dr. Dixie Melillo at the Rose Breast Cancer Center in Houston. He "interviewed" the staff at the center, telling them his wife had found a lump in her breast, that they had no insurance, but that he wanted the best care for her anyway.

The staff at the Rose Breast Cancer Center explained they don't turn anyone away, no matter what a person's financial circumstances, and Larry quickly learned that the center's medical reputation was right up there at the top. When the staff heard about the Darrs' situation, they didn't just send Larry out the door with instructions to bring in his wife; instead, they called Monica and told her, "You have an appointment tomorrow. We look forward to seeing you."

The next thing Monica knew, she was headed into surgery. After undergoing a radical mastectomy, Monica opened her eyes to find herself in the recovery room. When the fog of her anesthetic lifted, she saw her husband was right there beside her, along with her "old" friend Paula Garrett. (So old, says Monica, "We rode the same dinosaur to school together.")

Monica didn't ask about her prognosis, whether her life expectancy was long or short. And today it still doesn't really matter to her. She's living her life as though every day could be her last.

Her pal Paula brought her to a Women of Faith conference, where Monica told us she hoped she could stay out of the valley of cancer in the future. But at the same time, her experience there had taught her an invaluable lesson, one she might not have learned if she hadn't joined the ranks of the Valley Girls.

"In the valley, you're forced to look at your life and appreciate what you've got that's good. You find out that some things just aren't important," she said. "People get upset over things that don't really matter when you step back and look at the big picture. For example, I work in real estate, and sometimes situations can get pretty tense. But when emotions build, I tell myself, *No matter how this deal turns out, nobody's gonna die.*"

six

VALLEY PETS: ARF, ARF

l ife is a series of dogs." I read this quote by a comedienne in my morning newspaper, tossed my head back, and guffawed with recognition. If I wanted to help my sons think back on a particular memory, all I had to do was remind them which dog we had at that time and their memories were activated.

Our puppy roster started with a frisky beagle pup named Dudley. I don't even remember how it happened that we got Dudley; I just know that he was a bundle of energy, and he kick-started a lineup of dogs that would dance (and do other things) throughout our home.

But Dudley had an accident that forced him to learn to

dance on three legs. Actually, he did a bit of a jig. His disability never slowed down his enthusiasm for life and people, but in time, because of an undetected infection, Dudley had to be put down. During his stay with us, we also had two aquariums of tropical fish, a kitty named Moses, a parakeet, a turtle, a hermit crab, and a trio of gerbils (Shadrach, Meshach, and Abednego).

Dudley brought such joy that we didn't hesitate in welcoming Daisy into our family; she was a mixed breed with a sanguine personality. She bounded about like Tigger from *Winnie the Pooh*. Daisy presented us with nine puppies—all at one time. Eek! I ended up at the mall looking for good homes for those sweet, blond puppies, which people scooped up like vanilla ice cream on a summer day.

Then we took in a Russian wolfhound named Nadia. Nadia flinched and cowered anytime a man came into the room. It was heartbreaking, but it was also impractical with two sons in the house. Poor Nadia was a nervous wreck. I gave her to a gentle-hearted woman who adored her. I missed that dog; she was such a lady's pet. Even though Nadia was emotionally fragile, she was graceful, and when she ran, she was sheer poetry.

Next on our doorstep came Dusty, a German shepherd–husky mix. Dusty was handsome and had an agreeable personality but died young when he was struck by lightning during a sudden summer storm. That jarred us, but we were determined to have a dog for our sons, so we tried again.

Our next puppy was Tuesday, a cockapoo. This rough-and-tumble little fur ball would be with us for twelve years. She would take on man or beast yet was gentle and dear with our sons. Tuesday had several litters, and she was a wonderful mommy. Her puppies were easy to place in new homes, except when I accidentally gave away a little male who was returned weeks later when the new owner discovered the pup was only impersonating a boy dog. So "Fred" became "Fredda" and lived with us for a year before she was hit and killed by a car.

Did I mention Puppy? Puppy was the only deformed pup that Tuesday gave birth to. "Sidewinder" would have been a perfect name for Puppy because, when he ran, his backside kept trying to pass his head on the right. He was undersized and looked strange, but he was endearing. Puppy didn't live long, but he remains a sweet memory.

When Tuesday died after twelve years in our home, it was a sad day. Did I say "day"? We still miss her.

Our eldest son was in the air force when his precious pet dropped over, but our youngest was still home and soon wanted another dog. At Christmas we gave him a shih tzu that we named Pumpkin. Pumpkin lived thirteen years. She was loving and obedient—and mumbled a lot.

We aren't sure what Pumpkin was saying, but I hope it was a thank-you for loving her.

I was out of town when Pumpkin had a stroke and needed to be put down. My sons couldn't bear to take her to the vet, so my daughter-in-law did. Danya held Pumpkin while the vet put her to sleep. Thank you, Danya.

Yup, the comedienne was right: "Life is a series of dogs."

I think God put animals here on earth because they please him and because he knew they would make our valley life easier. It's not that they don't require upkeep; let's face it, they can be a handful and a wallet reducer. But they give so much more than they require—affection, protection, comfort, and enjoyment.

I have many friends who are either cat or dog owners. They all would testify to how much valley joy they have experienced because of their animals. Sheila's dog, Belle, is a bichon frise that twirls around in the living room like a ballet princess, breaking the hearts of neighborhood poodles for miles around. Natalie's dog Coco, who is no bigger than a ball of white yarn, jumps out of her traveling Poochi bag, runs and grabs her Poochi purse, and then jumps back in the safety of her "house," poking her head out the window for applause. It happens so fast you can hardly believe what you just saw.

Pat and Lana both have beautiful cats who have my

friends wrapped around their little paws. While these cats may not do tricks on command, they are in command. Trust me. Cats cuddle on their own terms, and even though they require you to sign a prenuptial, cat owners don't seem to mind.

Being a dog lover, I would pirouette backwards to have a dog. But since I spend so much time on the road, I'm relegated to enjoying other people's pets and stories about animals in books on my shelves. One of my favorite "pets" in book form is Brer Rabbit. He is that sassy, smart, and seasoned rabbit who loves living in a briar patch—a fact that saves his life, leading him to exclaim: "I was born and raised in a briar patch. Oh, my Lord, he's sure been good to me!" I love Brer Rabbit's story because it reminds me of the redeeming value of having been born and raised in brambles. Valley life is full of briars that can puncture us, or we can adapt, patch up life, and find refuge in the midst of piercing pain. And here's why: 'Cause our Lord, he's sure been good to us.

VALLEY VIEW

About 52.5 million dogs reside in our country. (I wonder who counts them!) Did you know that 60 percent of U.S.

households have at least one dog or cat? Or that the *Journal of Gerontology* has new research showing that the elderly are less lonely when they have regular dog visitors?

Because canines have forty times the number of scent-receiving cells in their noses than we do, dogs often distinguish themselves by using their noses, including detecting certain types of cancer by scent. And they are invaluable in rescue efforts. During the 2002 Westminster Dog Show at Madison Square Garden, twenty German shepherds were honored for their tireless work at the World Trade Center devastation. Each dog was introduced by name and received thunderous applause from an appreciative audience.

Countless stories have been recounted about pets that have saved their owners' lives from drowning, fires, and accidents. So, if you haven't applauded your pet lately, you might want to give him or her a rousing ovation—or a treat, which in my experience gets a more enthusiastic response.

VALLEY FRIENDS

My friend Linda daily celebrates her dog, Buddy; so it's not surprising that, when she was in trouble, he was there lickety-split. Here's how Linda tells the story:

One day I ran errands and returned to find Buddy obsessed with something in my pantry. He has been known to "stalk" mice in the walls, waking me up in the middle of the night as he tried to claw through them to get to one. So I thought it must be another mouse in the wall taunting him. That was, until I saw Buddy dive to the back of the pantry, and a large—as in gargantuan—rat came running out right at my feet. I'm thankful he made a sharp right and wiggled his fat frame under my shoe rack.

After putting on heavy boots, I pulled boxes off the shelves so Buddy could get closer to the rat. We could hear it scurrying and screeching, then it ran out and back again. Eek! This went on for about fifteen minutes, when Buddy made a lunge into the corner and came out with the screaming rat in his mouth.

It wriggled free and ran into my bedroom and under a small dresser. Buddy tried to get to the rat, and the rat screeched. Well, at least we knew where the rat was, but what was I going to do now? In a primal panic, I called Smithereen's, an exterminating company. I desperately told the receptionist of my plight, and about twenty minutes later, Larry pulled up in the white Smithereen's truck. Meanwhile, Buddy stayed on guard and kept the rat under the dresser.

We kept Buddy in position at one end of the dresser, placed a plastic tub at the other end, and then banged on the dresser. The rat screeched and thumped around. Buddy was going crazy but continued to keep the rat cornered.

I stepped into the kitchen for a second and then heard, slam, thump, thump, thump. When I ran back, the rat was in the plastic container.

While Larry gathered his things, Godzilla Rat bashed the top off the plastic tub, and I saw a foot and tail emerge. I screamed bloody murder, Buddy went crazy, and Larry slammed the lid back on the rat, thwarting its escape. We grabbed some packing tape and cocooned the plastic tub, sealing it shut.

I'm grateful for my golden "rat" dog, Buddy, who came to my rescue.

That performance, Buddy, was worth at least a tubful of doggie treats.

On another note, my friend Ney has a mixed dog named Bailey who not only rings bells at the back door when he needs to go outside and gives high fives, but he also is an unbelievable crooner. Bailey is especially passionate when performing patriotic songs, operas, and "Happy Birthday." One of my birthday highlights each year is when Ney, her housemate Mary, and Bailey call me on the phone to sing.

Ney also had a poodle named Pearl that, when asked, "Pearl, how much do you weigh?" would run into the bathroom and hop on the scale. What a brave little girl!

I stayed for a week as a guest in Ney, Mary, and Bailey's home last year. And I wasn't the only visitor. They were also hosting a guinea pig named Hamtaro while his owner was out of the country.

One morning I heard what sounded like anxious rustling and nervous whispers. Usually Ney and Mary are calm, peaceful gals—beautiful examples of grace under pressure. So I went out to investigate. May I just say that grace had been replaced with gasps?

It seems Hamtaro was missing, and they were frantic to find him. Neither Ney nor Mary wanted to tell the eight-year-old owner, Christian, that Hamtaro had hit the road or bit the dust. They kept thinking that the fluffy pet was hiding somewhere in his wood shavings, but neither of them wanted to look lest she discover a still-life form.

So I filtered through the bedding, but Hamtaro wasn't there. Then I checked the floor for Hamtaro droppings, which didn't take long to spot. The beaded line led north between the washer and dryer and then took a sharp jog to the east. I lay across the clothes dryer and looked down toward the floor only to find something staring back at me. It appeared to be a stuffed toy wedged between the wall and dryer atop a folded rug.

"Ney, are you missing a furry toy? If not, I may have found the prodigal."

Turns out the fluffy pet was stuck and eager to be retrieved. But even more relieved were the homeowners, who haven't stopped thanking me. Very sweet. I felt like such a hero.

Pets are the best, whether you have a canary singing the blues, a softer-than-down puppy licking your nose, or a book full of charming pet stories. Our valleys are sweeter because of them.

seven

VALLEY WONDER: WIDE-EYED

W-O-N-D-E-R, a six-letter word that means "that which arouses awe, astonishment, surprise, or admiration." The *American Heritage Dictionary* lists as an example the Seven Wonders of the World. I may never travel to the Seven Wonders, but quite honestly I can walk out to my backyard and be filled with awe.

No, I don't have a pyramid or a temple back there; why, I don't even have a hanging garden (unless you count that dandelion clinging tenaciously to the side of my house). Yet my heart is filled with awe when I examine the tatted lace of the Queen Anne that grows like royal

trim at the edge of a wooded area. I was equally astonished yesterday when, after a summer storm, a rainbow
arched across the heavens and appeared to pour into the
pond out back, turning it into a watery palette of pastels.

This spring I was surprised by two rotund toads that
had hibernated for the winter under a flowerpot perched
on our deck's railing. When I moved the container, I'm not
sure who was the most taken aback. The toads seemed to
cop an attitude, as if they weren't quite ready to give up
their reverie and I had gotten on their last nerve.

Then prehistoric birds landed in my front yard. Okay,
okay, so they weren't that old, but the sandhill cranes sure
looked like it. I was astonished at their height—I've never
trusted birds taller than I am. Their Star Wars squawk was
eerie, along with their disconcerting boldness.

Of course, they weren't any more aggressive than the
swallows on my porch that repeatedly dive-bombed my
head because I suggested they nest somewhere else . . .
like Capistrano. Yet I couldn't help but admire their
swooping tenacity.

Wonder is all around us: in a night sky, a summer
storm, a waterfall, or a tadpole's wiggle. It's definitely present in a baby's birth, the notes of a songbird's hymn, and
the gossamer beauty of a butterfly's wings. Wonder fills us
when a child utters his first word, when a baby bird takes

its first flight, and when our heart flutters with first love. And nothing compares to the wonder a mother feels when her baby moves inside her womb for the first time.

Friends of mine from the Women of Faith production crew, wanting to absorb some wonder, took a trip to Yosemite Park. Their goal was to climb Half Dome, an 8,842-foot-high mountain. The rocky hike was eighteen miles long. Several of the guys told me that everywhere they looked the vistas were breathtaking.

One of the hikers, Ed, had recently purchased a professional camera and was thrilled to snap pictures in an area so replete with wonder. Afterward he brought some of the exquisite prints from the trip into one of the conferences so we could see his shots of cascading waterfalls, giant sequoias, and panoramic mountaintop views. Below them in the Yosemite Valley were jutting rocks full of history, winding waterways, and meadows sprinkled with confetti wildflowers.

Tracking all that wonder to the top of Half Dome wasn't without cost. The hike took a lot of concentration and was physically depleting. One friend, Mike, shared that when he made it to an upper ledge just short of the top, he was so exhausted he lay down and fell sound asleep for an hour. He said he wasn't certain if he fell asleep or if he passed out, but when he woke up and assessed the last part of the trek, which was three hundred yards straight up using cables, he knew he had gone as far as he could. Mike said it was the most physically demanding thing he had ever attempted. But then he added, "I can't wait to go back."

Wonder seems worth it, regardless of the cost. I guess that's why folks travel around the world to see the Seven Wonders of the World for themselves.

For me, besides the wonder of my babies (sons and grandsons), I'd have to say my view from a mountain was the most wonder-filled experience I've had. Unlike my friends, I didn't attempt to hike up; instead, I rode up on a tram. Let me back up here and just say I don't do heights if I can help it. That's why I'm content to remain five foot in stature. My tiptoes are about as high as I care to go.

In fact, I just stayed in a hotel with an open atrium, which meant that when I came out of my room, I could look over the railing and see down into the lobby twenty floors below. Not only did I not look down each time I had to come or go from my room, but I also slithered against the wall while gripping an airsickness bag. When I initially checked in and saw my room, I wondered if in the night I would roll out of bed, out the door, over the railing, and find a new career as a desk clerk.

But back to my mountaintop experience. First I had to deal with this tram thing before I could worry about the mountain. I had never ridden in a tram because I never had attempted to go to a high peak. So the enclosed, itsy-bitsy buggy swinging on cables was the first hurdle in my escapade toward wonder. Actually, I wasn't looking for wonder when I climbed into the tram box; I just didn't want to give in to the flapping flamingo wings of fear in my stomach. As we boarded, I looked over at my friend Mary and mouthed, "Don't leave me!"

Where did I think she could go? The tram held sixteen people, and Mary coaxed me into the center of the enclosed trap—er, tram—while my friends encircled me. Wasn't that dear? My heart was going faster than the tram, but it soon evened out as my girlfriends chatted joyfully about all the fun we were having, which I had all but forgotten when the tram first took off for outer space. By the time we reached the top, I was glad I had gotten on.

Ever notice how often gladness is delayed?

I stepped off the tram and followed the others up a wooden ramp to a rock arch that opened onto the mountain. All was well until I looked to my left and caught a glimpse of how high I was. May I just say that even heaven isn't that high! All gladness dissipated as my stomach fell through my feet.

I didn't say anything. Actually, I couldn't. My voice box was in my stomach, which was now resting in the canyon below. I grabbed an inside railing and froze as I watched my friends walk away, unaware of my dilemma.

Self-talk is a wondrous tool—unless you're quarrelsome.

"Let go, Patsy, and move," I said firmly to myself.

"Fat chance!" I answered more firmly.

"You have no idea what's just beyond the arch—go for it!" I prompted in my best cheerleader voice.

"A slide . . . I just know it. I bet it's all downhill from here!" I whined.

Just then a young girl skipped past me. Skipped!

"Well?" I said accusingly.

"Well, what?" I replied snidely.

"Are you going to let a child show you up?" I taunted.

"I'm almost certain she's a prodigy; so yes, I don't mind."

I'm not sure if it was the child's liberty or the now deeply embedded splinters in the palms of my hands that motivated me, but I inched my way upward, all twelve feet, until I reached the safety of the arch. Then—drum roll please—I stepped out onto a wide place on the mountain of Masada, and my heart was enveloped in wonder.

The view of the Dead Sea from Masada was more than I could explain if I used all the adjectives in the dictionary. I couldn't stop staring. Luci walked up behind me and whispered, "Wait until you tell Les about this." And I thought, *But how could I ever explain it?*

I guess that's what wonder is: an inexplicable marvel, the sense you have when you're in the presence of something so beyond yourself. Quarrelsome me was temporarily speechless; I felt humbled by the sheer beauty of it all.

As I tried to memorize every watercolor inch of the view before me, the thought that reverberated within me was, *You almost missed it. You almost missed it.*

Having regained my voice, I replied to self, "But I didn't!"

When we left, I plastered myself on the far side of the ramp and inched my way back to the tram. As we boarded for the trip back down, Luci walked to the front of the tram right up at the window and said, "Come here, Patsy. Come stand with me."

And the strangest thing happened—I did. And it was grand, especially after I opened my eyes.

VALLEY VIEW

When have you gone in search of wonder? Where? What did you find? What did it cost you? Was it worth it?

Name three wonders in God's creation that thrill your heart just to think of them.

What is the most awe-inspiring thing you've ever witnessed?

Are you standing in a "wide place," or are you hemmed in by hardship? As you look around, what wonders do you see?

VALLEY FRIENDS

Sharon Lawrenz is a woman well acquainted with hardships. Her son Jared had been kicked out of school—again. Plagued with at least four major learning disabilities as well as attention-deficit disorder, eleven-year-old Jared never had been successfully mainstreamed into a regular classroom and never had fit in with other kids. His unruly behavior resulted in frequent disciplinary problems, and Sharon and her husband, Dick, had been forced to move him all around their city, struggling to find a new school that would take him after yet another one had expelled him.

"He was so bright as a kid," Sharon said. "He could play chess. He could walk by a thousand-piece puzzle spread out on the table and nonchalantly put five or six pieces in place as he passed by. But he had all these problems."

Jared exhibited a variety of unsocial behaviors, including being mean to animals. Sharon now knows his symptoms were classic signs of mental illness. But she didn't know that back then.

One spring day in 1988, when Jared had been expelled again, Sharon felt besieged. "Here was this precious son, the child we had prayed for repeatedly when I couldn't get pregnant for so long after our first son, Rod, came along. And yet our life was the pits because of Jared. He had never been invited to spend the night with a friend, never had been invited to other kids' birthday parties. He was miserable, and so was I, watching what was happening and not knowing how to help him."

At that moment frustration blended with resolve, and Sharon began a long, arduous journey of dogged research and unwavering commitment. She was determined to find Jared the help he needed, no matter where it was, and no matter what she had to do to get it. The journey was difficult, with no tram to ride, just a trip of anguish and hurt that led the whole family through a dark valley. During that time Sharon and her husband had to close their business, walk away from their unpaid-for home, file for bankruptcy, and move their family from Alaska to Los Angeles so Jared could be treated by professionals at UCLA and, later, be included in a successful drug trial at the University of Southern California.

After Jared's extensive testing, things started to change.

His preliminary diagnosis was borderline chronic paranoid schizophrenia; the final diagnosis came a short while later: Asperger's syndrome (a form of autism), obsessive-compulsive disorder, and anxiety. The diagnoses themselves were a terrible shock to these parents who thought they were dealing only with routine learning disabilities, but at least now they knew what was causing Jared's problems. Over the next few years, through lots more hard work and determination, they found appropriate schooling for him and the help he needed.

Not that there weren't setbacks along the way. Sharon, Dick, and their sons paid a high price, both emotionally and financially. Sharon and Dick's marriage nearly ended, and before long they found themselves falling on hard times again, with unemployment staring them in the face and Jared still getting into trouble, especially during his teenage years.

"I can't tell you how many times Jared got into trouble," Sharon said. "After I'd hear his side of it, I would say, 'So, if I call the school, am I going to get the same story as yours—or a different one?' And he would just sit there and hang his head. And I've had calls from the jewelry store, asking, 'Mrs. Lawrenz, did you *really* want to sell all this jewelry your son brought down here?'

"I was a tough mom, and I wasn't intimidated by my

child and his problems. I would tell him, 'I'm sorry you have an illness, but the world couldn't care less, and I have to make you able to survive in the world,'" she said. "And then there were those times when something bad would happen, and all I could do was draw him to me and cry with him."

Sharon and her family spent so many years in the valley it seemed for a while they never would see a mountaintop again. But now, looking back on those years, Sharon is awed at how God's hand was on them. "In absolutely amazing ways, he put us in exactly the right place at exactly the right time, and he provided exactly what we needed."

One of the wonderful ways God provided for Jared's family was by putting Joyce Smith in Sharon's life. The two became devoted friends, and Joyce proved to be a godsend to the whole family by encouraging Jared's parents and brother to seek counseling for themselves while they kept working to get help for Jared. Joyce's and Sharon's families became so close that when Joyce moved to Kansas several years ago, Sharon, Dick, and their boys soon followed.

There's so much more to tell about Sharon and her family's awe-inspiring journey, but instead, let me just jump up on a mountain ledge and trumpet the good news about their lives today. Jared, now thirty, lives independently and for several years has held a rewarding job at a home-improvement store. "He has his own truck, and he handles his own bills and medications and doctor appointments," Sharon said. "He's so happy. We're *all* so happy."

Their other son, Rod Lawrenz, an account executive with a technology firm, is married to Barbara, another Valley Girl whose story is shared in chapter 11.

Sharon's husband, Dick, is working full-time as a hospice chaplain and assisting Sharon with Pathway to Hope, an organization they founded to help families cope with the challenges of mental illness. Pathway to Hope, according to the group's mission statement, "exists to encourage, educate, and empower the individuals and their families whose lives are affected by mental illness."

"Dick and I said a long time ago, if we get this child raised and we're not wearing orange jumpsuits and locked up behind bars, we're going to help other people navigate this maze called mental illness," said Sharon. And that's what they've done.

In addition to heading the nonprofit organization, Sharon and Dick have also been professionally trained to lead eight-week courses, certified by the National Institute for Mental Health, for family members who have loved ones with mental illness. When needed, the couple serves as advocates for those families in their dealings with schools and courts, and Sharon has received additional specialized training to work with parents whose children require special-needs services in the school system.

Most recently, Sharon was appointed to the Johnson County, Kansas, Mental Health board of directors, and she also serves on a state board focusing on mental health. And here's a sweet note: last year she and Dick, a couple once on the verge of divorce, renewed their wedding vows after thirty-seven years of marriage.

Sharon's a Valley Girl, that's for sure; she knows what it's like to be mired in muck. But she also knows what it's like to feel God's presence, to experience God's wonder, even in that dark and desolate place. Today Sharon's bright smile and quick laugh light the way for others who are stumbling up the rocky maze that once intimidated Sharon and her family.

For more information about the services Sharon's organization offers to families affected by mental illness, visit www.pathwaytohope.org.

eight

VALLEY PLAY:
TILT-A-WHIRL PERSPECTIVE

*W*hen did I stop being excited about recess?

That question danced across the mind of my friend Leslie, who is an elementary school teacher, as she watched the children in her classroom run pell-mell out the door for recess.

Isn't that a great question? Most of us do lose that raw zeal as we grow older. The thrill of free time to swing, jump, and play can get lost in the pressure, stress, and responsibility of the grown-up world. And to some degree that's as it should be, but some of us take it too far.

Valley life is hard to balance. Work and play can be a

teeter-totter that keeps us either way up or way down. Remember as a kid how hard it was to keep the board in the middle? Then your partner unexpectedly jumped off, and with one fanny-smacking thud, you were definitely down.

As a young person I had a poor work ethic. My goal was to see how much work I could get out of instead of understanding how honorable it was to do my part and, if possible, to do more. I see that mind-set reflected in some young people today who hope they can snag a great job that doesn't require much of them. I listened to a young man recently who was bragging how he was able to lollygag in the back room and even take catnaps during his work hours. He boasted, as if not doing his part was a badge of honor and highlighted his ingenuity. A few fellows nearby agreed that it was their goal to find positions that required very little of them yet rewarded them with multiple benefits and a bulging bankroll. As I had, they sought what they hadn't earned.

My heart wanted to rescue them from that way of thinking, because I have learned the hard way it will rob them of self-esteem, a solid reputation, and the joy of accomplishment. Not to mention that when we are hard workers and difficult times hit our lives—which they will—we're far less likely to be paralyzed by them. When we have a strong work ethic, instead of shutting down, we have the mental moxie to push through the difficult times.

It took me time and much effort to go from dreading a hard day's work to finding satisfaction and joy in it. My whole mental approach had to shift. Today I've so teetered up from where I once was that I have to guard against the "all work and no play" syndrome.

Yup, it's tricky to find a healthy balance. Now my idea of play is to fit quick visits (via phone, e-mail, and lunch) with my friends into my cramped schedule. Or to boogie through a mall or sit long enough to peruse a magazine. Sometimes I play Sudoku or complete a crossword.

But where I have the most fun is with my grandsons, Justin and Noah. Those boys know how to play! And they still have enough child-wonder in them that they can make any place into a playground. A stick becomes a lizard, a robot, a laser, or a mustache. A stone is a toad, a dump truck, a roadblock, or a fortress. Their hands become airplanes, puppets, and monster claws. They don't allow the limitations of their surroundings to keep them from a good time.

How about you? Do you still remember how to play? If not, you may need lessons from a child. Watch the fascination in their faces when they examine a bug or their untainted imagination when they name the shapes of the clouds. "Oh, look, Nana, there goes a flying hippopotamus!" Check out the freedom they exercise when they roll down a hill. Okay, okay, rolling down hills may not be for us oldies, but we could do a soft skip through a garden.

I love to join little ones when they play with soap bubbles. They are thrilled over double bubbles or huge, iridescent ones that pop in your face, and they watch with anticipation the ones that fly higher than a telephone pole. What fun to introduce a child to the name of a flower or a bird. Yes, the spirit of a child keeps the valley lively!

In the same vein, my friend Leslie said she was watching her niece Danae listen to music on her CD player. Leslie observed how the young teen entered fully into every note, musical nuance, and word. It reminded Leslie of her own passion for music as a young adult, and she wondered when that had begun to fade. She's still young (fortyish) and a fan of a myriad of musical styles, but Leslie had lost the joy she had experienced when she took the time to listen closely and well.

Valley living needs music. It helps to tap our toes and lift our voices, whether in celebration or in a solemn ceremony.

When I visited Israel, we stayed the first couple of days in Tel Aviv and then moved over to Tiberias and then finally to Jerusalem. As we neared Jerusalem for the first time, our bus entered a tunnel, and our guide said, "Prepare yourselves, as we come out of the tunnel, for the view to your left."

We all wondered what that meant, and the anticipation built until, as we left the tunnel and pulled up an incline, a CD played "O, Jerusalem"over the sound system just as the view of the city appeared. The combination of the ancient site with the exquisite music was breathtaking. I wept. Many wept, it was so moving. I tucked the view and the music into a pocket near my heart to relive again and again.

Do you have musical memories?

As teenagers, my husband and I lived six hundred miles apart. What shortened that distance between us was the link of "our" song, "Are You Lonesome Tonight?" We're almost certain The King crooned that tune just for Les and me. Another song that became ours was sung by the Drifters—"Save the Last Dance for Me." Even typing the names of these songs brings a flood of sweet reverie.

This year I have the pleasure of sharing the Women of Faith Pre-Conference stage with award-winning singer Sandi Patty. She hits notes that rebound off the North Star and spill back over planet Earth, thrilling listeners. Not only can Sandi sing, but she also is very brave.

My singing voice isn't fit for public consumption, and

anyone who has stood within twenty feet of me knows this. It hasn't taken long for word of my off-key warbling to spread throughout the land. So when Sandi announced she had a song she wanted me to sing onstage with her and our singing friend Lisa, the Women of Faith staff were stunned and stumped. Where had Sandi been? We tried to bring her up to speed on my voice, but Sandi wouldn't hear of it and insisted this would work. The women in charge of our program looked stricken with concern. I was numb. Sandi just smiled.

Much to our relief, it turned out my part in the snappy song "Ain't No Mountain High Enough" was six spoken lines. The rest of the time I could lip-sync. (Although sweet Sandi assures me I can join in whenever I like. See, I told you she's brave.) Oh, and by the way, our trio does hand movements right out of the '60s while we sing, which makes me feel like a Supreme wannabe. Did I mention I wear rhinestone-studded sunglasses? The three of us will perform the song approximately forty-eight times through-out the year; so the music will be embedded within me.

What music is embedded within you? What do you find yourself humming? Perhaps a lullaby a parent sang to you or one you sang to a child again and again? Maybe it's a song you learned in elementary school ("Red River Valley," "She'll Be Comin' 'Round the Mountain"), Sunday school ("Jesus Loves Me," "Zacchaeus Was a Wee Little Man"), church ("Amazing Grace," the "Doxology"), or TV (the theme song from *Gilligan's Island*, Mr. Rogers's "Won't You Be My Neighbor?").

As I considered Leslie's musings on play and music, I wondered why I don't dance more often. As a young child, I walked from room to room on my tiptoes. It was my way of preparing for the ballet performances in my fantasy future. I also was a toe-tapper who tapped my way from one end of the house to the other in preparation for becoming a Broadway dancer. As a teenybopper, I was rocking and rolling constantly in preparation to marry Elvis Presley. And I got close when I married Les, who leaves me "All Shook Up" and has been serenading me for forty-four years. But guess what . . . he doesn't dance.

Maybe that's why I now listen to Andrea Bocelli. No dancing shoes required. But at unexpected moments my foot taps and my heart wants to pirouette. Then I get busy about many things and forget.

When was the last time you danced?

My friends Carol and Bruce, in preparation for the parents' dance at their daughter's wedding reception, signed up for dance lessons. Isn't that romantic? At that beautiful celebration, after they were introduced, they glided across the dance floor in each other's arms like Fred Astaire and Ginger Rogers.

King David was known to dance before the Lord. I wonder if he inherited that tradition from his ancestors. After all, Miriam led the women in dance after the people of Israel crossed the Red Sea (check out Exodus 14 for the full story). Of course, who wouldn't want to dance after hitting a watery wall and then suddenly realizing it's actually a highway to safety? That would put rhythm in even the most reluctant sandals.

VALLEY VIEW

When things in your life are going well, it's natural to play, sing, and dance. But sometimes in the midst of hardship and heartbreak, we most need to give ourselves a break. We all find it hard to participate in recess when our dreams have been crushed, to sing when our heart is aching, or to dance when we are soul weary. Yet sometimes a light-hearted touch, a composition of joy, or an unexpected twirl can diminish the tide of sorrow so we can catch our breath.

Last year our family went through some crushing blows. I could hardly breathe I was in so much emotional pain. I was confident of God's redemptive presence in the midst of our hurt, but that doesn't change that we still had to walk through the shadowed valley. I know how hard it is to lift one's voice to sing when it has taken all the strength you possess to lift your head off the pillow. Yet our singing anyway brought shards of hope. Even listening in to a playful conversation was resuscitating, and though I had no desire to kick up my heels, I found it consoling to be encircled in an embrace.

One evening when Les and I arrived home after running errands, we opened our car doors to hear music throughout the neighborhood coming from a nearby graduation gathering. The song playing was Patsy Cline's "I Fall to Pieces," which I found sadly appropriate for our situation. But without a word, Les took my purse from me and set it down on the driveway, turned toward me, slipped one arm around my back, and with the other took my hand in his. My nondancing husband waltzed me around and around under the stars. And I was deeply comforted.

VALLEY FRIEND

Years ago I met a woman who had been discarded by a philandering husband. He carefully had set a plan in place that would help him take full advantage of her financially before he announced his decision to move on to a younger woman. The wife never saw it coming and went into an emotional tailspin. Too dismayed to fight for her share of the monies and belongings, she was ordered by the court to move out of their home where they had raised their five children so the other woman could move in. She and her husband had worked hard for years to build a business, but he was given the company. She left their home and business with only a suitcase and a crushed spirit.

Their children were dizzy with confusion over how this could have happened to the family. Their main heartache was their mom. They worried that in her defenseless state she would become so despondent she would take her own life. The daughters checked on her daily.

One day they arrived and were stymied by what they saw.

Prior to the daughters' arrival, their mom was washing dishes when a love song came on the radio, filling the air with romance as she filled the sink with her tears. She cried out, "I don't even have someone to dance with."

She spun around to grab a tissue, and that's when she saw him. He was tall, somewhat stoic, but definitely available. She moved quickly toward him, wrapping her arms around his slim waist. They danced around and around, with her head tilted back and laughing with surprised delight. As she twirled, she spotted her daughters in the doorway staring, mouths gaping, like minnows in a pond. They thought their mom finally had cracked when they found her dancing with a broom.

The mom stopped and wiped away a few old tears. "No, I haven't lost my mind or my hope. Memorize what you've seen, because there may come a time in your life when you go through great loss, and I want you to remember to keep dancing."

Declare "recess" today and then sing until your heart dances with joy!

nine

VALLEY HOOPLA: DE-STUFFING STUFF

i wonder if one of the reasons valleys are so low is because they are weighed down with our stuff. After forty-four years of marriage, I've accumulated enough in my garage alone to fill the Grand Canyon. But I guess I'm not the only one; I read that in the United States last year we dumped about 330 million tons of garbage in landfills. How trashy is that?

Speaking of discards, one of my favorite trashy friends is Oscar the Grouch. If you remember, he lives in a garbage can on Sesame Street. When asked, "Why are you so happy?" Oscar answered, "Hey, hey, hey, I love the smell of trash and junk in the morning."

Well, Oscar, I could add to your morning's joy. In fact, you would be euphoric all day with my plethora of stuff that should be hauled to the curb. Truth be known, I'm a neatnik at heart, but "neat" now is buried beneath "jammed-in" because my stuff is having a population crisis.

What's the hoopla over owning stuff anyway? It doesn't really satisfy; yet many of us keep collecting as if the next purchase will do the trick. Then we will finally be content to whisper the benediction over all our stuff, "It is enough."

Instead, accumulating possessions seems almost addictive. Wait, did I say "almost"? It *is* addictive. Just ask the Home Shopping Network, QVC, twenty-four-hour superstores, eBay, and credit card companies.

Every time we toss another blue-light special into our shopping cart, we're signing on for the irksome task of keeping that item spiffy when we get it home. If we aren't shining, polishing, and dusting our purchases, we're repairing them. Stuff breeds the need for more stuff, complicating our lives with expensive upkeep and squandering our precious time.

So what's the cure? I'm not sure, or I wouldn't be knee-deep in books, greeting cards, and old letters. I'm trying to de-stuff and redirect my affections toward more worthwhile endeavors. And I keep meeting "stuff sisters" everywhere I go; like me, they're weighed down with their purchases. Perhaps together we can find the moxie to start pitching. I'll cheer for you if you'll cheer for me.

I have a hard time tossing things that either have long ago lost their sparkle or their usefulness. I keep thinking I might have occasion for them. As soon as I give something away or throw it out, that will be the very thing I'll need. Plus I'm sentimental, which is a stuffer's worst quicksand.

My fun-loving daughter-in-law Danya, who doesn't develop attachments to her belongings, just shakes her head at my chubby cupboards. She fears she'll be the one chosen at my demise to deal with my debris. I've tried to persuade her to another perspective. Some people have made cottage industries out of throwaway items, while others have art exhibits featuring creations made from discarded stuff. Danya doesn't think junk art is her life calling. Pity!

Perhaps, like me, despite your best efforts, your years of accumulation stick willy-nilly out of drawers, cramp your closets, and suffocate your storage areas. I can't tell you how many times I've cleaned out my closet only to have it jangle my nerves once again with its chaos in a week's time. Strangely, my overstuffed closet offers nothing to wear. Okay, that's not accurate, but even Dora the Explorer couldn't find all the parts to an outfit on my congested clothes racks.

Another location that constantly threatens my sanity is my desk. Where does all that paper come from? Did you know that the average person uses approximately seven hundred pounds of paper per year? When Rittenhouse and Bradford started manufacturing paper in the first U.S. mill in 1690, I'm sure they never imagined the paper trail they would inspire. I'm definitely over my weight limit. I worry that the paper police will show up to cite me. Why, I have seven hundred pounds sitting on my desk right now, and I'm barely into the new year. I have mountainous stacks of mail, notes, snapshots, magazines, telephone numbers, appointment cards, invitations, requests, projects, calendars, etc., etc., *et cetera*! (Excuse me, I didn't mean to scream, but I have a bad case of papyrus, which causes me to break out in et ceteras.)

To add to my accumulation—as if I needed more—when my mother died, I inherited her collection of belongings. Eek! Now I know where the saying, "Stuff doesn't fall far from the family spree" comes from.

Actually, by her seventies Mom had pared down, but what she kept was puzzling. I understood why she might want to retain a solitary cufflink of my dad's, who had died twenty-five years before, but I didn't understand the twenty-two empty plastic bear containers that once held honey. Or the fifteen broken broaches, or the packet of flower seeds dated "Use by June 1973," or junk mail from the 1980s.

That is, until I started going through *my* weird collection. I stump my own sensibilities when I tenaciously hang on to old photographs of people I don't even know, or awkward snapshots in which folks I do know are missing important parts of their anatomy—such as their heads. I have pictures of folks I don't like. Excuse me, but did I just say that aloud? I meant that I have shots of folks I haven't seen in eons.

I need to rifle through and thin out the pictorial ranks, which are pouring out of shoeboxes, trunks, and raggedy photo albums. I either need to dump some of these anonymous posers or to make up names and stories to keep the photographs interesting. Quite honestly, many of these mug shots are scary looking.

I've learned some important aspects of myself as I've tried to pry my possessions out of my own hands. I've realized that I become overwhelmed easily by disarray, by life being out of control. When I'm tired, even the multiple choices staring back at me from the grocery shelves can leave me dizzy and exhausted. No, I'm not saying all messies have the same source for their clutter as I do, but it does explain part of the ongoing drama I have to face when stacks of stuff need ordering or discarding.

Some folks need to own things they'll never use. I knew a lady who had hundreds of pairs of shoes, most of which she never wore even once. Hmm, now that addiction may require counseling.

Others are just plain procrastinators, which is a polite word for lazy bones. Or some may be indulgent and then harbor guilt because they know they have more than they need. Still others don't know how to effectively handle their belongings because they lack the skills to divide and conquer.

Grasping truth, such as what causes me to behave a certain way, helps me to gird up my mind against my feelings and to remind myself that "I can do all things through Christ who strengthens me" (Philippians 4:13), including cleaning out the excesses in my life. Still, even if I'm mentally shored up as I enter my closet to bring order, I can waver emotionally when it's time to actually toss.

I need help waiting for me in the wings, and maybe you do, too. Why not invite a friend or family member to help you sort and toss? Choose one who is a good throw-away-er and who has your best interests in mind. That way, when you hedge, she can pry your grasp loose. Besides, an objective person can bring a fresh breeze to your stale approach.

If we look at releasing our items as a way to bless others, that can help. You may know of some folks who would love to have you share your belongings with them. If not, Goodwill, Purple Heart, the Salvation Army, shelters, and other organizations know of scores of struggling families and individuals.

Then, of course, garage sales are an option. I would rather stick pins in my fingers than mark, sort, display, and sell my array of oddities. If someone looked over my stuff and then returned to her car empty-handed, I'd want to let the air out of her tires. I know that's tacky, but some of us stuffers are that way.

Yet many a gal who doesn't take it as personally as I do has accrued a good paycheck from putting her paraphernalia at the curb and selling it to those of us who can't pass up a deal and who recognize a "treasure" when we see one. If you have a favorite charity or an event at your church you want to support, you could donate your garage-sale earnings, which would add to your sense of achievement.

VALLEY VIEW

Scripture has some worthwhile thoughts for us to consider about our time and our stuff. Some of us have such a wall of accumulated stuff blocking our view that we lose perspective on what matters in this life. Pause with me and reflect on these:

"Don't hoard treasure down here where it gets eaten by moths and corroded by rust or—worse!—stolen by burglars. Stockpile treasure in heaven, where it's safe from moth and rust and burglars. It's obvious, isn't it? The place where your treasure is, is the place you will most want to be, and end up being" (Matthew 6:19–21 MSG).

"Set your mind on things above, not on things on the earth" (Colossians 3:2).

"If you live squinty-eyed in greed and distrust, your body is a dank cellar" (Matthew 6:22 MSG).

VALLEY FRIENDS

In Phnom Penh, Cambodia, stands a garbage dump nicknamed "Smokey Mountain" because the garbage rotting there creates methane that burns constantly. Surrounding this one-hundred-acre dump are makeshift shacks housing about two thousand people, including approximately six hundred children. The children spend the day digging in the garbage rather than going to school. They breathe in the toxic fumes as they help make money for their families, earning approximately fifty cents per day. And because of the monsoons, the children live and play in fetid water.

How blessed we are in America! We walk to our sinks and drink clean water, we set out our garbage at the road and others carry it away, and we sit down three times a day to dine. How can I be satisfied buying what I don't need when I know that people around the world don't have basic needs? Quite honestly, for a long time I tried not to think about world hunger, beyond praying for those who are hungry, because I couldn't imagine what I could do to make a difference. The problem was so big, and I was just one person.

Then I heard from World Vision (an organization that attempts to be Valley Friends to the helpless) what one person could do to help another, and it gave me a way to reach outside myself and all the way to the other side of the world.

For several years now I've helped to support a family of six in Ghana through a World Vision program. This family sends me messages of gratitude because they now have a healthier diet, supplementary clothes, writing pens, and even some toys. But I wanted to do more. Last spring I made a trip to World Vision headquarters in the state of Washington to attend a symposium. There I met, through film, people in third-world countries. On seeing the intense poverty, my heart broke, and I wept for two days, often burying my face in my hands as I heard first-hand accounts of children suffering around the globe.

Recently I adopted, through World Vision, a little Cambodian girl named Theary. The small sum I contribute every month goes toward her schooling and making sure she has food and clean water. I feel good about that, but I ache for the countless children who still need a helping hand. I want to do more.

Don't you?

What can we each do to order our personal world and to reach out to others? Let's work together to help the helpless. Perhaps we should start with a garage sale. I'll cheer for you if you'll cheer for me.

ten

VALLEY COMPANY: HOW SWEET IT IS

The Moon
There is such loneliness in that gold. . . .
The long centuries
Of human vigil have filled her
With ancient lament.
—JORGE LUIS BORGES

*h*ave you ever looked up at the moon, that solitary golden circle, and felt lonely? Me, too. The moon has a backdrop of stars, but they seem so distant, as if they had their own shiny-badge club, and she didn't qualify. Too round, I guess. Or perhaps the club disapproved of the moon's oft-worn mottled veil.

No doubt we all experience that sinkhole in our soul

called loneliness. It's been a part of the valley condition since the Fall. Why, even in the garden, God said, "It is not good that man should be alone" (Genesis 2:18).

I couldn't agree more. I've noted many men who, left on their own, tend to grow furry experiments in the refrigerator, not to mention on their faces. They manufacture bacteria farms in their shoes; and new virus strains form in the mounds of malodorous laundry. Not to mention that most men, if left unattended, would starve to death, get hurt trying to operate the dishwasher, choose not to attempt the rigors of an iron, and eventually, be eaten alive by herds of dust bunnies.

But, alas, I digress . . . back to loneliness.

Even in the company of my "Adam," at times I feel alone. Not because he's inattentive or not present. Why, I've felt waves of loneliness in an arena while in the company of twenty thousand other women.

From my experience, loneliness isn't necessarily caused by a lack of people but is more an inner ache caused by a fractured soul. The question, Is this all there is? rumbles through the corridors of our minds. *Shouldn't I be more? Do more? Feel more whole? Be more fulfilled?* Or perhaps we don't feel heard, understood, cherished, appreciated,—or maybe we just ache for our *real* home where one glorious day all our issues will be resolved.

Until then I thank God he knew we would gain comfort and joy in relating . . . usually. So he gave us each other. Have you noticed the recent surge of interest in celebrating friendship? Tons of cards, books, and clubs are devoted to friendship. And I've watched thousands of women over the years attend Women of Faith conferences dressed alike. Sometimes a hundred women will wear matching T-shirts—or tiaras. I love that. It breeds a spirit of camaraderie.

Girlfriends are so connected. We "get" each other. You know, the monthly cycle stuff, the flashes, and the moods from down under (and I don't mean Australia). I think we girls feel less alone in our feminine experiences when we can gab about them with someone who's having the same chaos in her anatomy. Guys just glaze over when we whine about cramps, water gain, or our hurt feelings, whereas women commiserate.

Commiserating is rooted in community. And community gives us a sense of people coming together for a common purpose. Now, that sounds friendly . . . unless you watch *Survivor* or *The Amazing Race*. I've noticed even members on the same team get on each other's nerves; yet let one of them be isolated or separated from "his people," and all he can think about is reuniting with the very ones who had frayed him. Aren't we a strange lot?

Loneliness feels like trying to waltz without a partner.

After my friend's husband died, when loneliness would press hard against her heart, she would pull out his suit jacket and wrap the arms around her body to ease the pain. I think that was a healthy way to seek a moment's comfort from her grief. But sometimes we find loneliness fillers that only complicate our lives.

Many of us seek solace in the refrigerator. We try to drown our lonesomeness in a friendly jug of caramel Frappuccino with a Blizzard chaser. We companion ourselves by getting up close and personal with a vat full of cheese sauce–slathered pasta. But instead of relieving isolation, we end up feeling not only lonesome but also loathsome. Even dancing alone becomes too challenging with the added tonnage weighing down our self-esteem.

Others of us try to cover our personal agony by talking too loud, too much, or not at all. Hiding in silence is a real door-closer to relationships. Some become braggarts, name-droppers, comediennes, and storytellers—as in whoppers. Others of us shop too much, work too much, sleep too much, or just plain *do* too much.

Have you noticed the repetition of "too much"? Anything we are doing too frequently needs to be examined, because that activity is often a smoke screen to cover our hurt, boredom, disappointment, and loneliness.

So what's the solution? For me, it helps to understand that loneliness is part of the human package and that connecting with others is vital for my well-being. Sometimes another person is just what the doctor ordered; at other times, people can be our greatest pain and the reason we need a doctor . . . of psychology.

Realizing that other folks weren't designed to be the final answer for our struggle with isolation keeps us from blaming them for our condition and protects them and us from unfair expectations. Friendships work much better when you understand what a person can and can't bring to the girlfriend party.

Years ago I attended a conference with a circle of friends. One of the activities was to place a press-on circle on our hand between our thumb and first finger. The circle changed colors according to how much vitality you had. Soon my friends' dots were glowing shades of blue, green, and yellow. Mine was jet black. According to the color scale, I had died, but no one had told me.

Then a friend, whose dot was a vivid aqua, took my hand. "Let me give you some of my color," she offered. Within moments I had drained all the color out of her circle, and now both of our dots were black. My friends all announced that I needed to try something new with my health regime.

I became defensive; they had hit a raw nerve. I had been on different programs through the years with poor results.

"Patsy," one of my friends said, "usually you're teachable, but when I mention your health, you're very resistant. It's almost as if you have given up hope of ever being healthy."

I excused myself and fled to my room. My feelings were hurt, and I was angry because I felt misunderstood. I had tried to make food and medicine changes, always with negative results, and I thought my friends were being judgmental. I saw them as insensitive because they didn't have my frail constitution.

When I reached my room, I fell on my knees and cried out to the Lord, "Get them!" I know, I know, that wasn't very nice, but it's what I said.

Then I reached for my Bible. When I opened it, my teary eyes fell on this verse, "Sing to Him a new song" (Psalm 33:3), and it pierced my heart. I was flooded with the realization that I had given up hope, but I needed to try again. My friends had been right.

I apologized to them and then went home and called a nutritionist to help me make some important changes. I'm grateful for friends who cared enough to confront me and then to step through the months and years ahead as my health took a gradual upward swing.

One way we can drain the color out of our friends and

put them into their own valley slump is to expect too much from them. Needy people aren't usually good company. No one wants to be in charge of another person's emotional condition.

I was labor intensive not only with friends but also with my dear husband. Because I had been fearful and frail for so many years, I had allowed others to do for me what I should have been doing for myself. So I had more changes to make than just my diet, as I learned to take responsibility for myself on many levels.

Sometimes we feel lonely because we are waiting for others to rescue us, and we are disheartened when they don't. But God didn't design other people to be in charge of our lazy bones. That's our job, with his help. He is our Deliverer, and he longs to be our closest Friend.

Of course, God does sometimes use others to rescue our lonely hearts. Only a few weeks ago I was in transit from an airport to a hotel when the driver and I had a conversation about a rescue that will stay with me for a long time. After the driver had loaded my suitcases and we had both buckled in, we headed for the hotel. We were cruising along in the middle lane of the freeway when I asked him, "So what fills your days with joy?"

"Oh, that would be the Man Upstairs who puts breath in my body each day," he responded.

"Great answer. Life is such a gift."

Suddenly the driver honked his horn in short, passionate blasts. It startled me and probably the drivers of vehicles around us, because I noticed they moved to far lanes and sped up. The man continued to honk and to point toward a car on the far outside lane. I glanced nervously in the direction he was pointing, only to see two older women driving and chatting, seemingly unaware of this young man's attempts to gain their attention.

He must have honked his horn fifteen times (yes, it made me nervous) before the woman driving looked over and saw him. A big smile crossed her face, and she waved.

Then he said proudly, "That's my baby."

"Baby?" I repeated, confused because the woman was too old to be his girlfriend or his child.

"Well, actually she's my aunt." Then, after a moment, he said, "My mother died. I was an only child. My aunt stepped in the gaping hole of my loss."

"How old was your mom when she died?"

"Mom was forty-two." He paused, then continued. "She was murdered. My stepfather shot her and then killed himself. That's when my aunt stepped in."

After a quiet moment, he pointed to her vehicle and whispered, "Yup, that's my heart driving that car."

What a tender statement of gratitude, birthed out of a

tragic loss. Thank God for women like his aunt who are willing to step in to be valley "company" to those unable to go on alone. Talk about needing a friend! Why, that man could have been bitter and withered in soul, but because of God's provision, I could see the light of hope on his face. I'm sure some still nights he wears a mottled veil of grief, but in the daylight hours he's pressing on.

The valley is tough enough without feeling you're on your own. Valleys, like the moon, are beautifully sad. Part of the beauty is that we can connect with others, which helps to ease the isolation. Part of the sadness is that we are able to miss the joy of companionship.

If you feel lonely because no one calls or includes you in their activities, you may need to look at what kind of company you are. I hope you'll take the time to think through the questions that follow. Perhaps you could jot the answers in the margins of this book. I think if we're honest, we could experience an important breakthrough in the way we relate with others, or at least consider a relational realignment.

VALLEY VIEW

Let's consider how desirable we might be as friends—but don't be disheartened if you dislike some of your answers;

we're all in process. These questions are meant to help you pinpoint some adjustments you might need to make in how you relate with others. Then again, you might love your answers and want to celebrate.

- Do people seek you out? If not, why do you think that is?
- Are you fun? Thoughtful? Interesting?
- Do you ask questions that draw out others?
- Are you an engaged listener?
- Whom do you seek out for company? What qualities draw you to them?
- Make a list of what you expect from a friend.
- Are your expectations reasonable? (Share your list with someone you respect to get her perspective.)
- List the qualities that make a person high maintenance.
- Which of these qualities do you exhibit? Are you willing to change? Jot down the first step you'll take.
- How many friendships can one have and maintain?
- How does one nurture a friendship?
- What does it mean to have boundaries (healthy lines) in a relationship? Are your boundaries in place?

- Has anyone ever stepped in for you? Who? When? Have you thanked them?

For me, I love a person who is well-read, life savvy, and tons of fun. But am I all that? The answer would be no. But, listen up; this is important: I'm working on it. God isn't looking for perfection, just progress. Measurable progress creates within us goodwill toward others. When we change for the good, it improves the way we feel about ourselves, and that improves how we interact with others, which brings about in them a desire for our company.

So, as I consider my list of "wants" in a friendship and then examine how I meet my own criteria, I would say that I'm a reader, and I've lived long enough to be fairly savvy, but am I fun? I've been known to communicate a funny story from time to time, but truth be known, I'm more serious than jovial. I have an intense personality, and I'm a bottom-line person, which means I can be jolting and weighty. I'm working on lightening up, and I'm practicing kindness more consistently.

Also, I lean toward being a selective lover, whereas God has called us to be like our Savior Jesus, wide-hearted embracers of people. I would be satisfied to like those I'm naturally drawn to, but God doesn't want to leave me in such a small space. I realize now that many people whom

I initially didn't care for have turned out to be important investors in my life. Left on my own, I would have missed out on some amazing relationships. Besides, I needed the honing they brought to my rough-edged character.

So, from my seasoned valley perspective, as I stumble toward becoming good company, I'd encourage you to expand your thinking by staying current in your reading, find reasons to laugh—it will improve your looks and perspective—and figure out a way to be kind every day . . . every single day.

VALLEY FRIENDS

On the outside, Lisa Nunez had a good life, maybe even a mountaintop life. She had everything going for her, but in her heart a valley of loneliness existed. She had business associates but longed for social pals; she had acquaintances but no one she could describe as a close friend.

"For a whole year, I prayed for more girlfriends," she said. "I have an older sister, Sabrina, but she has broken off ties with our family. I don't know where she is, and that hurts. I just really needed a friend, someone I could talk with and laugh with and do things with."

Lisa knew she wasn't going to find friends by staying

home alone; so she started looking for nurturing groups and gatherings. One day someone at church invited her to a new singles' group. "If you want to come, we're going to Sabrina's house," the woman said.

Hearing her sister's name jarred Lisa; she didn't seem to be able to get past the pain of that lost relationship. She associated the name with a hurt that was still fresh, a heart that was still broken.

But Lisa finally worked up the gumption to go, and, in God's mysterious way of working things out, Sabrina Calderon, who hosted the meeting that day, eventually became Lisa's close friend.

Shortly after that, Lisa met another woman, Sheri Meurer, at a different church gathering. After they crossed paths a few times, Lisa suggested they meet, just the two of them, for lunch.

"That way, if we ended up not having anything to talk about, it would be easy to excuse ourselves and go home," Lisa said.

She and Sheri talked for five hours—long after the lunch dishes had been cleared away and the staff had set up the restaurant for dinner. Eventually, the two women went back to Sheri's apartment and talked five more hours. A friendship was formed.

Lisa told us this story at a Women of Faith conference.

And guess who was sitting in the seats next to her? Her friends Sheri and Sabrina, of course. The three friends came together, and their easy banter and quick laughter showed the kind of close, comfortable relationship that was growing between them. They consider themselves "fortysomething sister chicks," and you can tell by looking at them they're Valley Girls, marveling in how God put in their lives what they needed. They just had to put forth a little effort and recognize the gift they had been given.

May I suggest that tonight, before you go to bed, you gaze up at the moon? Don't be afraid of your reflection. Go ahead and waltz if you like. And take heart that the moon may appear to stand alone, but look at it shine.

eleven

VALLEY PUZZLE: THE MISSING PIECE

O ne of my favorite childhood memories is coming home from school to find my parents leaning over the kitchen table at work on a crossword puzzle. The dictionary would be lying open with a short stack of encyclopedias nearby. Hot mugs of Maxwell House coffee spurred on my parents. My dad's pocketknife was at hand so he could whittle a sharp point on his pencil.

That pencil was poised in midair as Dad waited for inspiration to come to either him or Mom so he could fill in the empty squares. Graphite smudges on the puzzle meant he had made repeated corrections. If the puzzle was too difficult, Dad would make up the last words just so he could finish. Occasionally I would notice his creativity and mention the errors to him. He would grumble something about poetic license and shoo me away. That still makes me giggle.

My husband's mother, Lena, was also a crossword junkie. In the late-evening hours, she would hunker over a puzzle before retiring and then again over her first cup of morning coffee. Unsurprisingly, my husband has followed in her steps. Their preference was easy fill-ins so it could be completed by the time they emptied their coffee cup.

I, too, am a puzzle addict. I do crosswords sporadically, but I love Scrabble, picture puzzles, and Sudoku. More recently, I've tried Kakuro. If anyone would have told me that I would ever—and I do mean ever—enjoy number puzzles, I wouldn't have believed him. If I were oil, numbers would be my vinegar—we just don't mix.

During a long airplane flight, my friend Lyn introduced me, against my strong protests, to Sudoku, the Japanese number puzzle. Much to my surprise, I took a shine to it. Then my friend Randy slipped a book of Kakuro in front of me and dared me to try it. I was certain I couldn't manage the mental aerobics required, but lo and behold, I completed the challenge and even enjoyed it.

I think this means Jesus is coming soon. I mean, I've

always been stymied whenever two numbers get close to each other and I'm supposed to come up with a sum total. This numberless condition has been going on inside me for more than sixty years. Can a person with a blank chalkboard suddenly possess deciphering skills? Scary.

I'm perplexed—not just about my latest habit, but by people, too. I find them puzzling, don't you?

I don't get sunbathers. Isn't water a quicker bathing method? Slathering our bodies in oil and then baking until they are well done just doesn't add up to me. I understand that a fifteen-minute stint of sunrays is good for us, but I have friends who would spend every day sunning if they could.

Of course, I'd probably be out there with them in my itsy-bitsy, teeny-weeny, yellow, polka-dot . . . nah, never mind, I'm kissin' kin to the Pillsbury Dough Boy. I make Snow White look like a Fort Lauderdale beach babe. Besides, after a short time the sun causes me to blotch up like a beagle. Is that fair?

See, that's another puzzle to me: Why can't we all tan, ace classes, be athletic, play piano, paint with watercolors, and be entrepreneurial?

And what about folks who are rude? What's that about? Actually, some of them don't even seem to notice as they bulldoze along, leaving a trail of victims in their path. The other day a lady told me she didn't initially like me because I was short, old, and gray. As if I had a vote on those qualities. Why did she need to tell me that? To make my day? Surely she didn't think her perceptions would come as a news flash, did she? I mean, I have a mirror, and actually, when I looked up at her, I thought I was looking into one. That woman might have been all of an inch taller than I was, perhaps a year younger, and every bit as gray.

Yup, people puzzle me. Even people in the Bible . . .

What was Abraham thinking when he told a king that his wife was actually his sister? I think that was more than rude, because he put her in danger, which didn't seem like a husbandly thing to do. But then his wife, Sarah, didn't deny his claim. We girls tend to be that way—willing to bear up under duress to protect our husbands. And while that can be admirable, in all things boundaries need to exist, especially if our mate is putting us in danger.

I meet women all the time who are being abused, bullied, and degraded. It breaks my heart. That's not God's high calling for a woman or a man. God's love is tender, merciful, kind, and sacrificing. He never meant for men to badger, mistreat, or intimidate women. He designed a man strong to be a shield of safety for his wife.

Someone else who puzzles me is Eve. I mean, if you have perfection, why risk it all? Her husband was wonderful—even God said he was good—so she wasn't pining for a better man. Eve's home, the garden, was lush all the time because the weather was perfect and the water system was a balanced mist. The wildlife wasn't wild. All the critters were friendly—no biting mosquitoes, no stinky skunks, and no threatening beasts. Talk about a petting zoo—Eve lived in one.

If the animals were friendly, her husband was good, her garden was lush, no clouds were in her sky, and no rain appeared on her horizon . . . then why, Eve, why?

Yes, Eve puzzles me. But we don't know much about her life or her heart. Wouldn't you have loved being a mouse in her garden? It would probably fill in a lot of the blanks for us ponderers.

The list of puzzling people goes on. . . . Whatever possessed Jonah to run willy-nilly away from God's directives? Or Saul to lose sight of how God had hand-selected him as king? Or David to have Bathsheba's husband killed in battle? Why, people, why?

Indeed, that is a question worth asking myself. Why do I hold God at bay when what I long for—peace, love, and safety—are held in his hand? Why do I wonder if the Lord is trustworthy when he's proven himself over and over? Why is it easier to phone a friend than to call on Jesus? Why, Patsy, why? We're all a puzzle, aren't we?

Valley View

So how do we put together the pieces of life's puzzles that keep us confounded? Or do we? If I'm a conundrum even to myself, how can I understand someone else's jigsaw existence? We're so intricate, so layered.

The Bible cuts through intricacies, layers, and even generational influences and helps us to understand some basics about our human condition. For instance, we're told that those who hate being corrected are stupid (Proverbs 12:1). How clear is that? No riddle there: listen up or be a loser.

And we're told that a woman who causes her husband shame is rottenness to his bones. (Hmm, would that include Eve? Or was theirs an equal-opportunity sin? Oh, there I go again, puzzling.)

Scripture tells us that idle chatter leads to poverty (Proverbs 14:23). Is that referring to poverty of our spirits or is it financial? Perhaps it's both. Yes, yes, I'm sure it is.

The human condition begins to make sense as we glean the head-on truth of the Word, which is not to say that even if we were scholars people wouldn't perplex us or certain Bible verses wouldn't stump us. But when we receive what we *can* understand, it opens our understanding a little more, like one puzzle piece fitting snugly into another.

VALLEY FRIENDS

Barbara Lawrenz used to look at women in abusive marriages and wonder, *Why are they staying? Why don't they get out of there?* To Barbara, it looked as if those wives were in a valley situation they could easily leave behind. It puzzled her. But she has learned the hard way—by traveling through that valley herself—what keeps some terrified women in unhealthy and sometimes violent situations.

When her husband became abusive, Barbara did flee from her bad situation with her seven-month-old daughter, Faith. For a week they lived in a women's shelter, then moved on. Barbara spent years looking over her shoulder, hoping she wouldn't be found by the ex-husband who had threatened that if Barbara ever left him, he would find Faith and kill her.

Barbara settled in another state with kindhearted relatives who allowed her and Faith to live with them for a year while Barbara got back on her feet. When that year ended, she had to make other arrangements. Eventually she enrolled in a state university to become a teacher, qualified for financial aid, and moved into the campus's family-student housing. The decision to attend college was a gutsy move for a single mom who barely was able to make ends meet and who often wondered how she would feed her little daughter and provide a safe place where they could sleep.

That's when new understanding came to her about those women who stayed in abusive relationships. "They're in that bad situation, yes, but at least they know that their children are going to have food to eat and a place to sleep," she said. "I know now that's one of the big reasons they stay. Not to mention, it's sometimes easier to know where your abuser is and what he's thinking than to leave, constantly worrying that he's plotting to come after you and make good on his threats."

Barbara was in a dark and difficult valley, that's for sure. But several months earlier she had claimed Jeremiah 29:11 as her personal Scripture verse: "'For I know the plans I have for you,' declares the LORD, 'plans to prosper you and not to harm you, plans to give you hope and a future'" (NIV).

Throughout that long ordeal, "every time I was unsure whether I was making the right move, that verse would come to mind, or I would see it written on something," Barbara explained.

For example, when she enrolled in school, she had to find a new job in the small college town. She interviewed at a breakfast restaurant that had just opened near campus. "I had to push pretty hard to persuade the owners to hire me," she said. "My first day on the job, I walked up to the counter and found a card taped to the cash register. It was 'my' verse, Jeremiah 29:11. I knew right then and there that I was doing the right thing. In fact, the restaurant owners became my close friends—the only friends I had in that town at the time."

Barbara gradually began to fit the puzzle pieces of her life together, although she remained fearful that her ex-husband might reappear at any time. In 1999 she was married again, this time to a wonderful man who had been a family friend. Barbara and Rod had met each other at a family gathering ten years earlier, when they were both teenagers living in California. Rod legally adopted Faith, so Faith's and Barbara's last names changed, and Barbara could finally relax a little, knowing it now was more difficult for her ex-husband to find them.

She interrupted her schooling for a year when their son, Brandon, was born, and, for the most part, fear was replaced by joy. There was one new concern, however. Barbara's mother, Violet, who had moved to Kansas to be near Barbara and her new family, had endured multiple heart attacks and struggled with congestive heart failure. Periodically Violet ended up in the hospital.

During one of those hospitalizations, Violet was assisted by a student nurse who helped Violet maintain her dignity during a very difficult and stressful medical event. Barbara said, "When Mom was telling me how wonderful that student nurse was, I had a sudden inspiration that I was supposed to be a nurse instead of a teacher."

She had just finished the third of five years needed to earn her education degree, but, inspired by that student nurse's impact on her mother, Barbara switched majors and enrolled in nursing school. That same month, Brandon was diagnosed with severe autism, requiring in-home therapy for thirty-five hours per week. Barbara's mother and brother had arrived just in time to oversee that therapy while Barbara continued with her schooling. In 2003, however, Violet's health took another turn for the worse, and Barbara found herself in a valley of demands that included being a full-time student while caring for a special-needs child, raising a rambunctious daughter, helping a mother with health problems, and running both her own household as well as her mother's. Despite all those challenges, in 2004 Barbara became a registered nurse. She now works in a hospital's intensive-care unit, where her mother has endured several more health crises and is sometimes admitted for treatment.

Valley Puzzle: The missing piece

Barbara learned a few years ago that her first husband had died. She says now, "I wouldn't want to live out that bad time again, but I'm thankful I went through it. You see, when all the trouble started, I wasn't a Christian. In the middle of that really bad time in my life, I went up to the altar and accepted Christ as my personal Savior. From that moment on, everything started happening—very difficult, but ultimately very positive things—that led me to the safe and happy life I have today. God had a plan for me, and even though it led me into the valley, it has also led me out of it."

Barbara smiles now when she says, "My new husband and I have had some tough times of our own, including a period of unemployment. But I don't worry much. I especially don't worry about finances because I've been as low as you can go and gotten it all back tenfold. I don't regret the things I've gone through on my own or what we've gone through together. Those experiences have made me more compassionate, less judgmental—and very thankful to have Jesus as my Savior."

We met Barbara and her mother, Violet Johnson, and her mother-in-law, Sharon Lawrenz, at the national Women of Faith conference in Fort Lauderdale. (You'll find Violet's and Sharon's stories elsewhere in this book.) They had all the outward appearances of carefree, fun-filled, laughter-loaded, Lord-loving ladies. But there was something else about them—maybe something in their eyes—that made us recognize them for what they are: Valley Girls.

twelve

VALLEY FARE:
A GOURMET TREAT

i 've gone elliptical! No, not "ecliptical," as in out of this world, although I have been known to be a little spacey. "Elliptical," as in I'm taking long walks and getting absolutely nowhere—but I do sweat a lot. And to think I paid for this opportunity.

An elliptical machine is a low-impact exercise machine that doesn't put stress on one's back or joints. And the machine is working . . . actually, I'm the one working: it's people-powered. It doesn't move until I do. No motor, no free ride. The gliding motion, coupled with arm movements, is, I admit, a challenge. I can do it, but after only minutes, I know I've done it. The other day my six-year-old grandson, Justin, out-walked me on it. That was depressing.

My doctor's words motivate me to press on: "God made us hinged so we would keep moving." Then he added, "He didn't make us with roots sprouting out of our feet." I checked, and the doc's right—unless you count that corn on my little toe.

Not only has my exercise quota changed; so has my valley fare. That's because I've started a health program. (That's my way of not using the *d* word, which makes me break out in candy bars.) In fact, a number of my friends also went on the program with me because we believe misery does love company. And sure enough, when we were given our individual eating parameters, we were miserable.

Okay, let me speak for myself. When you deny me my cheese-laden pasta or chunks of butter-sopped French bread, I get surly. Surly is unattractive on a senior who is already estrogen starved. When food-denied and hormonally tipsy, I have all the potential of a cranky pit bull.

Learning to eat differently means one not only has to think differently but also shop differently. That's a lot of different. Isn't it Scripture that says, "Thou should not teacheth an old pit bull new tricks"? Perhaps not. Actually, it says, "Put a knife to your throat if you are given to gluttony" (Proverbs 23:2 NIV). Hmm, here's my question: Is it wise to give a surly, growling, estrogen-deprived woman a knife? Pause and think on that.

I have a hard time maintaining a regimen when I'm grumbling, so I had to make peace with this new approach to food. (Note my continuing effort not to use the *d* word.) I told myself I could learn to love other foods that were better for me. Do you know how hard I had to talk to convince myself that a rice cake is every bit as yummy as a caramel sundae?

Sometimes my inner cheerleading helped me, but other times I was just downright crabby, which I know wasn't fair to those around me. More than once I had to apologize to my husband for being short with him when what was really bothering me was that I wanted the bowl of buttered popcorn he was face-first in.

For some reason food has become more important to me as I've aged. Maybe that's because as a person "matures," physical activities tend to be cinched in a notch or two, leaving some of us overly focused on the table. Food seems to become a replacement for physical activity. And it certainly is a social focus.

If we don't watch out, food can become a reward system. I've overheard myself saying things like, "Patsy, if you clean out that drawer, it should be worth at least a small soft-serve cone." Now, how calorie-laden is that kind of thinking? Imagine if I cleaned the whole house . . . Ben and Jerry had better lock their vats!

What surprised me most about my new program was that when I stayed inside the recommended boundaries, it worked. Oh, I didn't lose all the weight I wanted to, but within weeks I felt healthier and my energy level improved dramatically. It was wonderful.

Yes, "was."

After three months I became lenient, and then I moved into downright indulgent. Phooey.

The good news is that I can begin again. That's the gift of a new day, a new hour. Mess up one meal, and we can improve on the next. Sounds simple, and it can be, unless I sabotage my own success, which, by the way, I'm gifted at.

Here are some things I find get me back on track with my valley fare. I hope by listing them I can flame both my own fire of motivation as well as yours—not that any of you need to improve your eating habits. (Okay, some of you *are* in the same fat vat I'm in.) Let's talk turkey—which, by the way, is a good, low-fat food choice.

First, I find I do a lot of mindless eating. I pick up whatever is handy as I jitterbug through the kitchen and pop goodies in my mouth without thinking. To curb that habit I have to watch what I leave out on the counters and even monitor more closely what I have tucked away in the cupboards, lest I go from mindless to obsessive when I kick into my snack mode.

I've learned not to go grocery shopping without a list, or I'll try to stuff the pasta aisle into my cart. Also, I must never shop when I'm hungry. Have you ever wanted, in the middle of a store, to rip the cellophane off a pie and gobble up the blueberry filling? Just checking.

Also, because I travel almost every week, I have to have a plan in place for the road. It's an effort to stay prepared, but it enables me to avoid the dash-in-for-fast-food attacks at the airport. I've found a few acceptable snacks I keep in my purse to ward off those panicky moments. Even chomping on a piece of gum can help me jump the hurdle of cravings.

Later in this book I talk about how my increased water intake has vastly improved my health. I can't tell you how much difference it has made. Water acts as an appetite suppressant as well as helps to support the body's entire system. From hair, brain, stomach, skin, eyes, digestion, to elimination, water is imperative for our well-being. I'm told that many health issues are caused or are seriously complicated by dehydration. Trust me, it takes a serious act of discipline for me to drink water, but I have so benefited from this new habit.

God's Word has a lot to say about valley fare, but the one word of counsel that's hardest for me is "moderation." Moderation smacks of self-control, discipline, and restraint. Ugh. That's hard. I enjoy second helpings, dessert after every meal, and decadent fare, which is exactly why I had to go on a program. When left on my own, I'm excessive. I need accountability, boundaries, and ongoing education.

Knowing good info doesn't necessarily keep one from making bad choices, but it sure helps shore up right choices. Part of the program we were on included teaching us how our bodies function best and how to make choices that support that information, which was very helpful . . . but still required ongoing discipline.

Scripture repeatedly reminds us of the importance of moderation and discipline. Proverbs is bursting with insights regarding our behavior and our choices.

Proverbs 13:3 reminds us, "He who guards his mouth preserves his life, but he who opens wide his lips shall have destruction." Hmm, I guess that could apply to our appetite for food as well as our tendency to blather unnecessary words. Who doesn't have to guard her mouth when ordering off a menu or when deciding whether to indulge in a dessert? When we don't exercise caution, we can set ourselves up for the "destruction" of unbalanced blood sugars and excessive weight that threatens our arteries, hearts, and legs. Yes, guarding our mouths is good counsel.

And what about Proverbs 19:15: "—an idle person will suffer hunger"? That "idle" business would explain my added weight during vacation. I end up thinking about what I'll be eating next before I've even finished what's in front of me. I guess that's why productivity feels so good; not only do we accomplish a lot, but the activity also keeps our minds off our appetite, which can be triggered by boredom and idleness.

You know when my appetite is most ravenous? At night. Not good. I am least likely to be active in the evenings and therefore don't counterbalance food intake with movement. I've also noticed that if I go to bed with a full stomach, I don't sleep as well. I'm told that during sleep our bodies do most of their repair work; so it's important we get our rest. Now, I've heard that all my life, yet I still need to be reminded.

. Valley fare can be eaten with flair. A lovely plate, a sunny placemat, and a handsome glass feed my senses and provide a portion of the pleasure that comes in sitting down to eat. My plate might not hold mountaintop food, but I'm concentrating on keeping my bones dancing. How about you?

VALLEY VIEW

Some folks don't seem to need as many Post-it notes as I do when it comes to caring for their bodies. Take Old Testament Daniel; discipline could have been his middle name. In the book of Daniel we read that he and his three friends were prisoners. They weren't offered measly bread and water, but instead rich fare—the king's delicacies and wine—was laid out before them. And these guys refused the spread. Huh? I wonder how hard that must have been to say, "No, we'll stick with veggies and water, thank you."

Listen, if I'm depressed or restricted, just feed me. The words "Don't eat chocolate" make me ravenous for that brown liquid oozing down mounds of mocha ice cream. Yes! Oops, I mean no.

On their self-imposed diet (eek! I used the *d* word), Daniel and his friends excelled in their health and their jobs for the king. They were impressive. So what do these determined men offer us that we can slip into our take-out bag to feast on later?

1. Have a menu in mind that's workable wherever you're eating.
2. Just because something is considered a delicacy and is available doesn't mean we have to eat it.

3. Discipline pays off with health and energy benefits galore.

I've lost and gained enough weight to be totally impressed with folks who, like Daniel, keep their food fare in perspective.

Valley Friends

Daniel's menu was impressive. Just listen to the qualities he and his friends exhibited: "Young men in whom there was no blemish, but good-looking, gifted in all wisdom, possessing knowledge and quick to understand, who had ability to serve in the king's palace, and whom they might teach the language and literature of the Chaldeans" (Daniel 1:4).

Wow! May I just say that again? Wow! Talk about scrutinizing an applicant. Those folks would have been in so much trouble with the Civil Liberties Union. How many of us would have qualified? Not me, I know that. But Daniel did. He was not only gorgeous and competent, but listen to this: "Daniel had understanding in all visions and dreams" (Daniel 1:17).

After Daniel was promoted repeatedly, the king and

even his enemies said, "Then this Daniel distinguished himself above the governors and satraps, because an excellent spirit was in him; and the king gave thought to setting him over the whole realm. So the governors and satraps sought to find some charge against Daniel concerning the kingdom; but they could find no charge or fault, because he was faithful; nor was there any error or fault found in him" (Daniel 6:3–4).

Impressive. But perhaps you're wondering what that has to do with food. Well, Scripture tells us that if we're faithful in the little things, God will give us more (Matthew 25:23). When Daniel and his friends refused to indulge their appetites, motivated by their desire to honor God, he blessed them. He gave them favor even with their enemies and kept them safe and fruitful in hostile surroundings. Also, Daniel's consistently good decisions strengthened his character. We see his source of strength as we read, "In his upper room, with his windows open toward Jerusalem, he knelt down on his knees three times that day, and prayed and gave thanks before his God, as was his custom since early days" (Daniel 6:10).

Perhaps I need to spend more time in grace and less time with my fork in the pasta bowl. Pray longer, eat less. Want to join me?

"Give us this day our daily bread. . . ."

thirteen

VALLEY DELIGHT:
GRACE-BASED HEART

*r*ecently at a Women of Faith Association meeting, Luci Swindoll was acting as moderator for a question-and-answer time with the speakers. Luci's ability to ask creative and thought-provoking questions made me look forward to the session. She didn't disappoint.

"Patsy," she asked, "I know you have a passion for writing and reading. If you had to choose to do only one, which would it be?"

"Oh, Luci," I said with a groan, "that's a hard one." I thought for a moment and then answered, "If I was forced to make a choice, I would choose to read, because when

I write, it's about what I know, but when I read, it's about what I can't imagine."

I guess that's why my old bones jiggle with new life when I enter a bookstore. I can't explain it, but with each step I take into the book-laden aisles, I breathe more deeply, and delight sets in. In fact, it happened just the other day when I was in Calgary, Canada. My book buddies, Marilyn and Pat, passed me in the hotel lobby, stopping just long enough to give me directions to a bookstore they had discovered a block away. Within minutes I stepped into the most wonderful three-story bookstore. The charming atmosphere was right out of a writer's dream. I wanted to set up my desk and live there.

And recently I was in the children's section of a large bookstore in search of a title. As I scanned the books' spines, I became aware of the eyes of a child on me. After a moment, the eyes sprouted a mouth that asked, "Can you *read*?"

I looked down into the delightful cherub face of a girl about five years old, who had lively dark eyes.

"Why, yes, I can," I answered with a grin.

"Oh, good. Then here's the plan . . ."

I could hardly contain my giggles. This little gal had a plan, which included me, a stranger. I couldn't wait to hear what she had in mind, and she couldn't wait to tell me.

"You're going to sit on that bench over there, and I'm going to sit on the step. Then you're going to read to me."

"Oh, I am? What am I going to read?"

"I'll get it." With that she pirouetted around to a nearby shelf, extracted a thin volume, and did jetés on her way back.

"Okay, sit down." She pointed to the spot on the bench where she wanted me.

Here's the funny part: I sat down. Something about this child made me want to obey.

Once I was in my place, she sashayed over to a step to perch for the performance. Then, just as we were about to begin, she stood up and announced, "And it's okay with my mommy." (As if I believed that one.) She sat down and gave me the nod to commence.

I was several pages into the story when her mom came in search of her little dumpling. When Mom stepped out from the aisles and spotted me reading, I stopped, looked up at her, and then confessed, as I pointed at her daughter, "She told me to do this."

The mom rolled her eyes knowingly, as if this was a regular occurrence.

I quickly interjected, "Your daughter has wonderful leadership skills."

"Oh, really?" she said crossing her arms. "And here all this time I just thought she was bossy."

"Oh, no, trust me, this energy, properly directed, could rule the world."

I walked away from that encounter with a lilt in my step. Obviously the mom was challenged by her little girl's strength, but I was fascinated with that child's spunk and inspired by her zeal.

That incident reminded me how a different perspective can help us to look at someone in a fresh way. Have you ever misjudged or underestimated anyone? Of course; who hasn't? We jump to conclusions, misunderstand, or sometimes limit those we know best. I guess it's that age-old struggle of not being able to see the forest for the trees.

Take the disciple Peter, for instance. Based on his wild-child behavior, I would have sent him to the drugstore for some Ritalin. Whacking off ears, boasting, sinking in his insecurities—Peter was emotionally all over the map. So imagine my surprise when Jesus calls him "a rock." I didn't see that one coming. The Lord must have been delighted to call Peter out of his obvious weakness into God's stunning strength by giving him a new name, Rock, designating Peter as a steady place to stand.

And what about Thomas? I mean, there was a disciple who needed to go on a job search. Obviously he didn't have what it would take to walk in faith. Yet Jesus allowed his doubting disciple the opportunity to touch his wounds, that he might heal Thomas's fractured beliefs.

Remember the woman who touched Jesus's hem and was made whole in her body? Imagine touching his nail-pierced hands. I have a feeling that Thomas, with the memory of our Savior's wounds tingling on his fingertips, never doubted again.

Then, of course, we have Judas. We all know he needed to be fired. Or did he? Surely the Prince of heaven knew Judas's heart. I mean, there's no way, when Jesus is calling the Pharisees to task for their dirty hearts, that he didn't see the filth in Judas. Yet Jesus allowed him to stay and stray. (I guess that sometimes, even when we can see something is very wrong, it doesn't mean that God isn't at work executing a much greater plan.)

I wonder how many times I've misjudged a situation—or more important, a person. Quite honestly, I don't think I want to know. But I wonder if I had any idea how wrong my judgments were, if that would help me to break the habit of thinking I know things I can't possibly know.

When I was traveling in Tiberias, everyone in our tour group was asked to pick up a small rock and to board a boat, which were replicas from the disciples' time. Then we made our way to the middle of the Sea of Galilee, and our vessels were roped to each other. Pastor Chuck Swindoll stood at the front of one of the boats and delivered an inspiring sermon. He concluded by asking each of us to take the rock we had brought and allow it to be a visual for something we needed to let go of. When we were ready to say to God, "I release this," we were to drop the rock over the side of the boat into the sea.

Seated nearby me was a scowling woman who evidently didn't like the assignment. I had noticed throughout the sermon that her brow was furrowed, and she couldn't sit still. Apparently she had no plan to do business with God that day. I secretly wondered why she had come along if she was going to close off her spirit to life-giving truth.

Dismissing thoughts about her, I got busy with my own business, and after a while I dropped my rock and heard it drown in the sea. The moment was moving, not just because of my release, but because I could hear the *plop, plop, plop* of other rocks being dropped from the surrounding boats. For a brief time the Sea of Galilee became the Sea of Sorrows, as it drank in our pain. Afterward it became the Sea of Celebration, which we, the relieved recipients, delighted in.

My furrowed "friend" held on to her rock, turning it over and over in her hand. I figured her mind was on the upcoming meal or on how long she was going to have to wait for the rest of us to dump our rocky "issues." But then, much to my amazement, she tossed her rock with gusto into the brink, and a smile smoothed out her brow. As we stepped back onto shore, I heard the woman say in a hushed tone to her husband, "We may need to get me some more rocks."

And here I thought she wasn't responding. Now I wondered if her furrows were caused not by disinterest but by the realization that she had accumulated so many miseries that one rock wasn't going to be adequate. Why, I had totally misread that burdened woman. The one thing I had done right was to stop judging her and to consider my own burdens.

Valley View

- Are you on the Sea of Sorrows or the Sea of Celebration? What put you there?
- Whom have you hemmed into a small space with your judgment?
- What can you do to change that?
- Have you experienced someone's judgment?
- How did that make you feel?
- When did you forgive them?

- If you haven't forgiven them, what would it take for you to be willing to drop your rock?

Valley Friends

Violet's journey through the valley began when she was forty-seven and woke up one morning with a numb finger. "I kept massaging it, but it was asleep, and it felt so cold it was almost like it was frozen," she said. "I thought, *I can't go to the ER with something as minor as a numb finger*, but then it starting hurting, so finally I gave in and went to the hospital."

The hospital staff found no pulse in Violet's finger. What they *did* find was a blood clot in her arm. The situation was so serious her finger eventually had to be amputated. But here's the good thing that came of this. Well, not everyone would think of it as something good, but to Violet, it led to some amazing mountaintop experiences. The medical staff's efforts to find Violet's blood clot led them to perform an ultrasound of her heart, which revealed what they thought was a tumor but turned out to be a hole that had been there since birth. To repair the hole, surgeons told Violet they would have to hook her up to a bypass machine, remove her heart and fix it, then put it back in her chest. There was a 20 percent chance of failure, but no other choices were available for realistic treatment.

Violet survived the surgery, and just as she was recovering from that valley, another one appeared when her marriage unexpectedly ended, and she and her husband of thirty-one years were divorced. She knew she had to find a way to support herself, so she enrolled in college to earn a degree she could use in forging a career for herself.

Her first major heart attack came at the end of her first semester. That was ten years ago, and since then Violet has had at least a dozen more major attacks and a round of kidney failure. She is kept alive these days by dual pacemakers and five stints, and more than once during Violet's various hospitalizations to have those surgeries and procedures, her family has been summoned for deathbed good-byes. Twice she has been brought back to life by CPR.

Maybe you think Violet is still in the valley, given the multiple times she has been "fine one minute and on my way to ICU the next," as she puts it. You might expect her to be a fearful, bitter woman who has withdrawn from an active life, knowing that each breath could be her last. Instead, she's one of the merriest women you'll meet.

And just where *did* we meet Violet? At a Women of Faith conference, of course! She was there laughing and crying and singing her heart out with the rest of us, enjoying every boisterous minute.

Here are the God-given thoughts that govern Violet's attitude today: "Every day I live is a birthday for me, something I celebrate as another miracle. I set little goals for myself, and when I reach each one, I celebrate and set another one. God puts little things before me that I need to live long enough to do."

That's how Violet has been living for the last twelve years: celebrating each new day as a miracle and reaching for that next goal. She had a number of opportunities to allow the bitterness that judgment brings to fill her broken heart, but she chose to move forward in her life and trust God. Violet is definitely a Valley Girl, but today she's a mama on the mountaintop, refusing to let her circumstances pull her down.

fourteen

VALLEY PARADE: MAIN STREET MARCH

i love a parade! We valley people need them to change our pace, brighten our landscape, and add some toe-tapping music to life's humdrum. I'd rather attend big ones like the St. Patrick's Day Parade and the Rose Parade via television because I'm not much on snarls of traffic and mobs of people. But for the little parades I like to show up curbside. Kids who wrap their bicycle wheels in crepe paper and neighborhood pets who prance about in cardboard hats please my small-town heart.

In fact, I even love the preliminary preparations when our family meets up at a designated spot, and then we walk together down to Main Street to pick out our little patch of earth. We spread out our blankets, set up a few tattered lawn chairs, and pass out bottles of chilled water. We slather the little ones in fresh doses of sunscreen, break out the sunglasses, and eagerly wait for the "doin's" to begin.

Speaking of doin's, I just returned from our hometown Fourth of July parade. What a hoot! Children did spectacular jump-roping feats; politicians pumped hands; floats, uh, floated; shiny red fire trucks blasted their screechy horns; panting dogs on new leashes wagged their long tongues and short tails; a fencing class with épées drawn fenced their way down Main Street with shouts of "Touché"; a few men and women on polished Harleys sported leather, tattoos, and American flags; and children on brightly decorated bicycles pedaled furiously.

But the highlight of the parade for our family was our grandson, six-year-old Justin, who walked sprightly along with his Tae Kwon Do class waving at the crowds like professional paraders. Nothing makes a parade more festive than when you have someone you love in the midst of it.

Oh, did I mention that two fighter jets sped over the parade with their sleek machines in perfect unison? It was impressive, but Justin still gets my vote for grand marshall.

Have you noticed that Scripture paints many parades for us to watch and take notes on? Probably none is more memorable than the exodus lineup of Israelites wearing their brightly threaded robes and Egyptian jewelry, herding flocks of sheep and goats, and carrying possessions on their heads, in carts, and on their backs as they marched out of captivity. With their faces full of fresh liberty and their feet ready for a steady departure, imagine how they felt when they had barely gotten out of Dodge and found the Red Sea roadblock looming before them and the Egyptian army in their lightning-fast chariots bearing down behind them. Now, that could squeeze all the dance out of a parade quicker than a thunderstorm. But Moses, the grand marshall, raised his staff and with it opened up an alternate parade route.

From the Red Sea to the desert and eventually to the Promised Land, the people argued, moped, fought, worshipped, and rejoiced. They had all that it would take to pull off a memorable parade—dancers, tambourines, singers, children, and craftsmen. And memorable it was, for all these centuries later we're still talking about it.

What was your favorite part of that parade? The manna? The battles? The tablets? It's hard to decide, isn't it? Especially since the walk covered forty years of life's ups and downs. The Israelites were in a valley, all right.

I find myself returning to thoughts about Moses and his people repeatedly because I can see that they, too, had times when they spun around in joy and had seasons when they could barely limp to the next location. I can watch and be encouraged when they struggle and fall down in the desert sand, because then they get back up (always with God's help), brush themselves off, and start over again.

Have you ever thought of your life as a parade? Try it. Mentally stand back and scan over the last year. Any highlights? Of course there are. Any weeks float by your mind that you would change or that you would like to redecorate? Uh-huh, me too. And we are not alone.

Take Jonah, who threw his own protest parade made up of a series of poor choices. First, he chose to ignore God's direction; second, Jonah actually believed he could escape the Lord's presence; and third, he tried to hide in both the lower part of the ship and a deep sleep to escape his responsibilities. After God's creative intervention, Jonah changed direction. I'm certain, in hindsight, he would have taken an alternate route.

Jesus had a parade of folks follow him around everywhere he went, none more noteworthy than his disciples. Some of them were rough and rugged, while others were tidy and slick. What kind of float would depict some of these men?

Take Peter. What could we use to capture his wild

faith? Hmm, his float would definitely need animation. He had a kind of Superman approach to life and faith, but with Inspector Clouseau results. Remember when Peter whacked off that guard's ear, or when he stepped out on the water to meet Jesus and then started to drown? Or what about when he bragged about the strength of his faith only to turn around and repeatedly deny Christ?

Yes, we need animation on this one for sure. I think of a float depicting Christ's great hand safely holding a rumpled young boy, slingshot in hand, with bandaged knees and a smudged face, who is leaping up and down trying to snag a wormy apple off a tree. That might capture an essence of Christ's compassion for Peter and for us as we attempt to be grown-up.

What about Judas? How does one depict greed, deceit, and betrayal? Perhaps we could have a purse made from a black shroud that released moths each time it opened. Lurking in the valley shadows nearby, a beady-eyed shrew would sit atop a single corroded coin. It wouldn't add joy to the parade, but it could be a solemn reminder of what a self-serving life produces, which is something we all need to recall from time to time.

We can't leave Paul out of the parade. What a colorful character! Like Peter, this float needs an action figure to capture Paul's flair. From persecutor to passionate follower, this zealot lit up the landscape with conversion contro-versy; so maybe on this float we should have some noise-makers. I know, we could have Paul being shot out of a cannon, holding his letters to the churches, followed by a great spray of fireworks. Too much? I think "too much" describes Paul to a *P*.

Then there's John. How could one capture Christ's beloved disciple? What about a newborn lamb coiled up asleep in a shepherd's lap? Or perhaps a man napping at his desk with a moist pen lying next to a parchment of the partially written book of Revelation. Imagine being called "beloved." Go ahead, imagine it, because—put on your dancing shoes—you are.

VALLEY VIEW

Okay, our turn. Shall we design our floats?

Let's see . . . mine would have to include dancing shoes on wooden feet to represent all the times I wished I had danced in the valley but didn't. Wonderful rhythmic music would play over the float's loudspeakers as inspira-tion for others to cut loose while they can and dance, dance, dance. . . . And trust me, I would join them.

What's on your float?

VALLEY FRIENDS

Twenty-year-old Sara George had been considering enlisting in the military, so she wasn't surprised when some marines paraded up to the Texas home where she lived with her parents, Penny and Carson. Sara thought the men might be recruiters who had come to talk to her about joining up.

For Penny, however, the marines' appearance was an awful moment now frozen in time. With one of her sons already serving in the active military; the other son serving as a police dispatcher; and her husband, a Vietnam veteran, away in Iraq working for a civilian contractor, she didn't know what to think when she saw the uniformed men standing at her door.

"I was just numb," she said.

The marines bypassed the unsuspecting Sara and courteously headed for Penny. They verified her identity and then continued with the words every parent dreads: "We regret to inform you . . ."

The Georges' middle child, twenty-two-year-old Phillip, a marine serving in Afghanistan, had been killed.

Phillip had first visited the marine recruiting office on September 11, 2002. His interest came as a surprise to his family, Penny said, "because my husband had served in the army, not the marines, and also, as a child, Phillip was the one who was fearful and shy. He wasn't the type you think of when you think of the marines." But he enlisted and seemed to thrive in the new, demanding environment.

"He was in boot camp when the military was first deployed to Iraq," Penny said. "Then he spent two and a half years at a base in Hawaii. He joked about doing his tour in paradise."

Penny said that his military friends told her that during his time in Hawaii, "whenever Phillip spoke, everyone listened, because he was quiet and didn't talk a lot. But when he did say something, they knew it was going to be either profound or funny."

Many times when his marine buddies had partied too much during the weekends, Phillip was the designated driver who hauled them safely home.

Phillip went back to Texas to visit his family in spring 2005, and a few weeks later his company of marines was deployed to Afghanistan to carry out a dual mission: delivering food and water to Afghani civilians and chasing al-Qaeda out of the mountains.

"They had just finished taking food and water to some children and were waiting at the landing zone to be picked up by the helicopters when they were attacked," Penny said.

Only one marine was killed in the attack—Phillip.

Can any valley be darker than the one that engulfs a parent whose child dies? Yet even in the midst of her devastating grief, Penny has found glimpses of sunlight peeking over the far-off mountaintop. Some of these godly glimpses have come in the kindnesses bestowed on them by friends and strangers alike during their heartbreaking ordeal. For instance, Penny said, when Carson's employer in Iraq heard the news, his colleagues arranged for him to go to Germany, where he was allowed to fly on the military transport plane that brought Phillip's body back to the States.

"That meant a lot to us," Penny said. "And before the flight left Germany, a female airman asked Carson, 'Would you like a little time alone with your son?' That helped him, too; he needed that time."

The transport plane first landed in the States at Dover Air Force Base, Maryland, and then commercial airliners completed the final flights home to Texas. Changing planes in Philadelphia, Carson sadly watched as Phillip's flag-draped casket and that of another soldier were carefully loaded into the cargo hold.

"Each time the casket was moved," said Carson, "it was done with so much honor and dignity that my heart swelled with pride in my son, and at the same time, it held such unbelievable pain."

Sitting on the plane surrounded by chatting passengers focused on their business or vacation plans, Carson must have felt like the only one whose heart was broken. Then the pilot made an announcement. "Ladies and gentlemen, we have the honor today of escorting home the bodies of two fallen heroes."

Carson didn't hear the rest. His heart was too full of swirling emotions and grateful thoughts that someone had acknowledged his son's sacrifice.

In the weeks and months after Phillip's death and the subsequent memorial services, some of Phillip's friends made long trips to Texas to visit his grave and to tell their fellow marine's family how much his friendship had meant to them. Those visits have been additional kindnesses for Penny and her family.

Penny prays that the way Phillip lived his life might have influenced the young men and women who served with him. "I would love to think that maybe he had a chance to talk about his faith," she said.

As of the time of this writing, Penny's husband has returned to his job in Iraq; her other children are returning to "somewhat normal" lives. For the most part, Penny is left at home alone. But she doesn't spend much time feeling sorry for herself. We found her at the Women of Faith conference in Houston, singing her heart out with the worship team, laughing at our silly moments, and wiping away tears during the poignant stories. She's a Valley Girl now, someone who can see how God helped her through that most difficult of places, still feeling his hand on her life at every turn. "It's God and my church friends and family that get me through each day," she said.

She wears Phillip's dog tags wherever she goes. They clink against her chest to acknowledge the pain she feels but also to show her pride in this son who, as she says, "completed the mission God gave him and then was called home." Her husband adds, "Praying to a Father who understands the pain of sacrifice offers us a strength unsurpassed by anything else."

Penny George knows the pain of that hard, dark place when a child is lost. But she's determined to live her life heading toward the mountaintop, always looking for a way to show a little gesture of kindness to someone else who has tumbled down into the valley of loss.

fifteen

VALLEY WATER: SIP OF SALVATION

i 've never been a water drinker. It's too, um, wet. Actually, drinking water makes me nauseated; besides, my body has never required much in the way of liquids. Or so I thought.

Our bodies can go to amazing lengths to survive even when we don't treat them well. Now I realize that my body was parched and withering from lack of moisture. I was in thirst-a-tion (Patsy lingo for "Water the hydrangeas, honey, the petals are falling off"). My body had been screaming for water, but I was so used to being parched, I didn't pay attention.

Some of us require a nudge toward the river's edge; I needed a mighty shove. I was ushered toward valley water when I started the program to improve my health (remember, it was a "health *program*"). I was dragging my wagon around at a snail's pace and needed to find a way to put some zip into my step.

I knew going into the program that I'd have to begin a light exercise routine, but what I didn't know was that I'd also be required to drink a cistern full of water a day. If I'd known that, I would have been reluctant to dive in. I think it's counterproductive to walk around the block with Lake Erie sloshing around inside, especially since that water is looking for a way to escape. But not being one to, ahem, whine, I learned to preplan my brisk walks to keep me within running distance of a privy.

We're all a bundle of habits, but among mine you wouldn't find consuming liquids, so it wasn't simple to revamp my thinking. Actually, it was like trying to convince a ripe pear not to fall off a tree.

The doc said that I needed to start off by sipping water off and on throughout the day. When I did, what happened surprised me. Not immediately, but eventually, I was drinking as many as eight glasses of water a day—four glasses before noon and four more by 7:00 p.m. That was a miracle just short of Niagara Falls. The results were impressive, as my body began to function better. My digestive track became kinder, my aggravated sinus condition settled down, and dry patches of skin smoothed out. I can honestly say all that water has proven to be refreshment for my health. Why, even the sprinting I now have to do to find Port-A-Potties throughout the land has been aerobically good for me.

Purposing to make change takes diligence. I had to consciously remind myself to drink water every hour, and then I did it whether I felt like it or not, at least most of the time. Retraining, while tedious, pays off in unexpected ways. Not only did my health improve, but I also felt a fresh infusion of self-respect flood in. Doing the right thing causes us to stand taller, dance more often, and step into life with more confidence.

In time, drinking water became a natural rhythm, but I noticed that, when my schedule became congested, the easiest thing to neglect was the latest addition to my daily routine. So during hectic times I leave myself notes on the fridge ("Drink, woman, drink"), I set out bottles of water to keep them visible and convenient, and I ask my husband to hold me accountable (preferably without lecturing).

On my recent trip to Israel, I cut back on my fluids because we spent hours every day on a brand-new tour bus without, I repeat, without a restroom. (A dehydrated man must have designed that rig.) At the end of the third day, I discovered my ankles had collected enough fluids that I could have replenished the Dead Sea. I began to flush my system with water, and by morning my watermelon ankles had returned to their original design.

No doubt about it, our bodies need water. I kind of wish we were more like camels—oh, not for the spindly legs, knobby knees, or penchant for spitting, but instead, for their capacity to hold water. Then we could reserve, say, Tuesdays for dipping our heads into a trough and lapping in our weekly supply. Alas, it isn't so. Rather, we must prod ourselves daily to drink up so we don't dry up and blow away.

Our spirits also need watering—from the well of God's Word. Just as our bones dry out and our throats parch, our inner lives become brittle without life-giving moisture, which drinking in Scripture provides. When I immerse myself in, say, the book of Philippians, it's like a cool draft of water that supplies me with the moisture truth brings.

I guess I shouldn't be surprised that water is so important to us. When I open the Bible, the first thing I discover is that in the beginning "the Spirit of God was hovering over the face of the waters" (Genesis 1:2), and then I read in the last chapter of Revelation that there is "a pure river of water of life, clear as crystal, proceeding from the throne of God and of the Lamb" (Revelation 22:1).

Between Eden and eternity there are many references to water, but my very favorite water story in Scripture is the woman Jesus encountered at the well. Wells in Bible days were a daily meeting place where women filled their jars while exchanging stories, travelers refreshed their strength before moving on, and animals had their thirst quenched. So in some ways it served as a social center as well as a place of practicality.

When Jesus approached Jacob's well in Samaria, he was weary from his journey, so he sat down by the well and asked a Samaritan woman to give him a drink. She was taken aback because the Jews and the Samaritans didn't interact. "How is it that You . . . ask a drink from me?" she inquired (see John 4:9).

Jesus replied, "If you knew the gift of God, and who it is who says to you, 'Give Me a drink,' you would have asked Him, and He would have given you living water" (John 4:10).

The curious woman leaned into what Jesus said, trying to wrap her thirsty mind around his moisture-laden words. He then ladled this invitation to her lips: "Whoever drinks of the water that I shall give him will never thirst. But the water that I shall give him will become in him a fountain of water springing up into everlasting life" (John 4:14).

The woman knew she wanted this water, but first Jesus exposed her past so she would understand more deeply the well she would be drinking from, the only well that could replenish her withered soul. When the Samaritan woman went into the city, she told the men that a stranger had told her "all things that I ever did" (John 4:29). She didn't presume to tell the men who Jesus was, but she posed the question each of us must one day consider for ourselves: "Could this be the Christ?"

The men rose up and went to see for themselves. She who had drunk in Jesus's words had whetted their shriveled hearts.

One statement in Scripture about this woman particularly captures my interest. After speaking with Jesus, the woman "left her waterpot" (John 4:28). You don't leave your waterpot behind in such a dry land unless your thirst has been quenched. I wonder if the vessel represented the way she had tried to relieve her wild thirst for love (five husbands and a current live-in), but now that she had swallowed true salvation, she abandoned her empty pot and hurried to tell others about this satisfying Jesus.

Are you thirsty? Or have you gone on such little water that you don't see the desert your scorched soul is living in? I invite you to join me in the Valley of Water at the well of his Word. Together we'll sip and recover from our arid ways. I've found the more I sit at his well and drink, the more natural it is for me to go there first instead of sprinting for my old waterpot of stagnant answers.

VALLEY VIEW

One definition of a valley is "the extensive land area . . . irrigated by a river system" (*American Heritage Dictionary*). The valley has a water supply that keeps it fruitful. Likewise, if we are to be lush and productive, we need a river to run through us. Partaking of a Bible study, whether we do it on our own or with others, will start the irrigation.

Lately I've been spending a lot of time in the book of Judges in the Old Testament, drinking in the refreshing water of truth that God calls us, just as he called Gideon (and the woman at the well), to be more than we ever dreamed. Imagine that.

Gideon was full of fear, yet God called him a mighty man of valor. God didn't extract Gideon out of his woes but instead watered Gideon's life right in the midst of enemies and chaos. Gideon would grow into his valor.

It doesn't matter how insecure we feel, how feeble our

résumé may appear, or how many times we've botched up our lives; God has a higher plan for us, and it begins with his wellspring within us.

I recommend sipping from John 4:1–30 and Judges 6–8.

VALLEY FRIENDS

Like many of us, sisters Jeanetta Ellis and Brenda Ripley have a load of emotional baggage that has pulled them into a valley perspective. At various points in their lives, desert winds have swirled around each of them—dealing with a parent's alcoholism and drug addiction and the resulting emotional abandonment, with sexual abuse by a family member, with medical emergencies, with a too-early marriage and parenthood, with the too-early death of Brenda's husband due to Lou Gehrig's disease, and the list goes on.

They have plenty of excuses for staying in the desert and wallowing in their sandy circumstances. Instead, they chose to use their valley experiences to water each other's souls. One of the ways they do that is to enjoy Christian women's conferences together.

That practice started back in 1992 when they received a flyer in the mail describing an upcoming gathering hosted by Lana Bateman. Lana is an experienced Christian leader who is especially talented at helping victims overcome the effects of sexual abuse through her own work and through referrals to talented and devoted Christian counselors. (Lana now travels with Women of Faith as our chaplain.)

The sisters read Lana's flyer and mused that it might be something they could use. So they went together—and wouldn't you know it, the first speaker was a feisty little woman (me) who talked about sportin' a 'tude.

Since then they've been regulars at various Christian conferences, including Women of Faith. "God has been freeing us from the baggage we're carrying," Jeanetta told us. "He's used others' lives and others' wisdom to help us get through what we've endured. And he's used Women of Faith. Every time we come, we're amazed to hear one of the speakers address something we're dealing with at that time."

Jeanetta and Brenda have a lot in common with so many others who have felt God's hand in the midst of dry places. Their godly attitudes keep them looking for ways to hydrate joy instead of grief, laughter instead of tears, forgiveness instead of bitterness. And in the midst of their bone-rattling hardships, they dance. They are Valley Girls ready to encourage others toward a well-watered faith.

sixteen

VALLEY DIRECTION:
TWIRLING WEATHER VANES

*W*hen we stepped out of the mall's doorway onto the sunny street in Calgary, my friend said, "Turn right."

"No, we go left," I replied.

"Nope, we go right. Trust me."

I wanted to trust her, knowing I had made a number of wrong turns in my life, but I still felt as if we should go left. After some friendly banter, I finally caved in, and we turned right. Sure enough, right was wrong.

But it ended up that what I saw was worth the extra blocks in the wrong direction. At the end of one of the blocks, towering metal sculptures filled the air. They were like great open loops slightly bent, which provided a graceful arch over the road. I thought they existed to add artistic flair to the cityscape. Later I found out differently.

When I returned to my hotel room, I noticed a book of photographs on the desk. As I casually flipped through the pages, I spotted a picture of the iron sculptures and learned that they were mandated wind shears. The tall buildings in Calgary's downtown created a wind tunnel, which caused high wind danger at the pedestrian level. The sculptures "attenuate," or weaken, the wind. In other words, without the structures, you could go shopping and blow a bundle, then walk out the door and get blown off your feet. That would be a trip to remember.

When my friend Carol received the wind-shear news flash that she had cancer, she turned neither right nor left. Instead, she sank down onto her knees and then slid onto the floor. I think she wished at that moment that she could be blown into the sky like a kite to wander capriciously above the doctors, chemo treatments, surgery, and radiation.

But that didn't happen. Carol pulled herself up and wobbled into her reality. Somewhere in the wind tunnel she stopped wobbling and finished the medical race at a sprint. Today, while Carol's feet are planted firmly, her heart is as light as a kite, kept aloft by her gratitude.

Life has wind-shear potential, no doubt about it. Lofty challenges and soaring trials that can knock us over with their velocity. Sometimes the wind brings bad news, such as a threatening health diagnosis or the loss of a job, and at other times it can be mind-blowing good news, such as "Surprise, you're pregnant!" All of these news blasts hold the power to sweep us over.

Johnny had worn Coke-glass-thick spectacles since his twenties, which interfered with many activities he wanted to participate in. Through the years he lived with the visual displeasure of his thick lenses and his limited vision, and he eventually gave up hope that the situation could ever change. Then Johnny developed cataracts, which seemed like a final blast to his vision.

Now comes the part that blew Johnny away. When his doctors performed surgery to remove the cataracts, his vision was restored. He could throw his awkward glasses to the wind. No more weighty spectacles and no more sight limitations. Johnny, who is now seventy-four, is seeing clearly and walking on air.

This past weekend I was in the green room of an arena when a gal approximately forty-five years old came in to stock the sodas and water. I greeted her and asked her how she was, to which she gave the courtesy reply, "Good, thanks." I didn't think she sounded convincing, so I asked her if she was *really* good or just *sort of* good.

She turned and looked at me. "I think it's a miracle that I'm walking and talking. My son was murdered three months ago, and sometimes I think I'm going to lose my mind."

What an honest answer. My heart ached for this broken-hearted mother who couldn't make sense of someone shooting her son in the back of his head while he was walking down the street. I knew nothing I said could bring reason to this act of violence, so I asked her if I could just hold her for a minute. Immediately she was in my arms. Sometimes the most comforting thing we can do is touch the grieving person—with his or her permission, of course.

That kind of mind-blowing loss not only knocks you off your feet, but it also has the potential to keep you pinned down for a long time. I was proud of this Valley Momma for getting up, dressing, and stepping back into the circle of life. She has a long, windy trail of grief ahead, but I know she's going to make it, one difficult step at a time.

VALLEY VIEW

- When was the last time you learned lessons from taking a wrong turn?

- What did you learn?
- What gust of wind swept you off your feet?
- What problems would you fly over if you could?
- What has been your hardest loss? A person? A dream? Finances?
- What steps are you taking to stay in the circle of life?

Make a gratitude list and keep it somewhere you can refer to when you're in a directional muddle.

VALLEY FRIENDS

When Claire Sites attended the 2005 National Women of Faith conference in Fort Lauderdale, she never dreamed that her ride home would result in a life-changing event.

Claire and three of her closest friends were at the arena when the doors opened for Thursday night's roof-raising kickoff session, and they were back on Friday for another eight hours of worship, praise, inspiration, and fun.

Then came the ride back to the hotel.

Claire's girlfriend Angie was driving the minivan, and the friends were laughing and recounting their favorite events of the day, taking delight in all they had experienced. "We were on a well-traveled, four-lane road, heading back to our hotel, which was near the beach," Claire recounted. "Then a rock came through the closed passenger window and hit me in the right eye."

The rock shattered the car's window as well as the plastic lenses in Claire's eyeglasses. "Instantly everything went black, and I yelled, 'I've been hit! Pray for me!'" she said. "Because it was a facial injury, blood was everywhere. But the Lord was with me and immediately took on the pain for me; otherwise, it would have been beyond bearing."

Claire's right eye was destroyed, and her eye socket and nose were broken. Somehow her friend Angie stayed calm enough to drive the minivan to a lighted area, while one of the other friends called 911. Then they all joined together in some mighty prayers.

"I felt the effects of those powerful prayers. It was such a comfort. It felt like those warm hospital blankets that are so soothing," Claire said.

The police and paramedics were there almost instantly. As the ambulance rushed Claire to the hospital, she asked the young paramedic who was tending her what his name was.

"Layton," he answered.

"Layton, I'm going to pray protection for you. I know

you're going to be working all night, and I'm asking God to keep his hand over you," Claire told him.

"Thank you, ma'am," Layton answered. Then he asked, "How did this happen?"

Claire explained that she and her friends were coming home from the Women of Faith conference when the rock had been thrown.

"My mama's going to that conference," Layton told her. "I'll be calling her as soon as we get you to the hospital."

And with that, a huge prayer chain began, linking Claire's home-church friends, the students and colleagues at the Christian school where she taught art, and a host of prayer partners she never had met who heard about her situation through Layton's mama and her many church friends. During her recovery, Claire received cards, calls, and e-mails from hundreds of people who had been praying for her; she even got e-mails from China and Thailand.

During the next year, Claire underwent two operations, including reconstructive surgery to rebuild her face. "For a while, I looked terrible because my bad eye was much lower, had sunk in, and was discolored. My husband had some glasses made with a dark lens to help me hide the eye."

Claire knows all about that dark, old valley—yes, she does. But listen to what she says today: "God is so good!

I was out of work for about eight weeks, but by the first of May I went back to teaching a couple of hours a day so I could finish out the school year. I have a hatbox stuffed with probably five hundred get-well cards. I call it my love box. And at school, the little ones still come up to me and tell me, 'Mrs. Sites, I pray for your eye.' One little boy asked me recently, 'Which one is your fake eye?' It's nice to know he couldn't tell."

Through an amazing set of "circumstances" (which Claire knows is actually God's role in her recovery), she had reconstructive surgery at one of the top-ranked eye hospitals in the world, and as an artist, she was amazed to learn all the steps that went into making her prosthetic eye. She jokes and calls it her "teenage eye" because "it never gets bloodshot, never droops. My other eye shows my age, but my new eye is wide-awake-looking; it always looks good."

Not that everything's all sweetness and light these days. Claire has experienced some temporary depression due to injuries from the accident as well as nerve damage to her face and mouth. She also has sensitivity to loud noises, a reaction her counselor attributes to post-traumatic stress disorder. But she's coping with her disability, reminding herself and others, "When I get to heaven, I'll have two good eyes again."

One of the first things Claire did when she awoke from

her initial surgery was to ask those who had come to be with her to pray for forgiveness for the unknown person who threw the rock. That forgiveness has freed her to see God's plan in turning her tears into testimony.

"God positioned me," she said. "He truly uses ordinary people to do the extraordinary for his kingdom." He's using Claire these days in the encouraging talks she shares now with women's gatherings and other groups. She's a Valley Girl, and like so many of us, Claire's sportin' a bit of a 'tude. She says, "How stupid is Satan? I'd just come through eight hours of praise and worship at the Women of Faith conference with 16,500 women, and he thinks a rock thrown at me is gonna take away my joy? I might be a target, but I'm not vulnerable to his misguided attacks."

Claire has determined not to allow her calamity to throw her off track or to blow her away. Her faith is acting as a wind-shear attenuator, just like those sculptures that filled the Calgary sky. Women like Claire cheer on the rest of us, showing us how to move forward regardless of how stiff the winds might blow.

seventeen

THE MOUNTAINTOP: AT LAST

*h*ave you ever gone somewhere you didn't particularly want to go, only to discover after arriving that you had waited all your life for it?

That's what Israel was for me. While I was delighted to join my friends for a journey, I wasn't certain how I felt about the Holy Land. In my mind, London and the theaters and tea in fine china cups sounded more like a good fit for me. Or France, with the quaint outdoor cafés and delicate croissants. Or Tuscany with its lavender highlights, dripping in delicate olive oils and tables crowded with colorful bowls of handmade pasta. Yes!

I'm into ambience, can you tell?

But when I arrived in Israel, I was fascinated at every turn. The ancient land imprinted itself on my soul. I hadn't expected such a wealth of agriculture, the contrasts between kibbutzim life and the nomads' desert homes, and the deep work of excavation compared with the scaling heights of mountains. I can't fully explain it, because the experience went deeper than words, ambience, or landscape. It was like an old song that I had forgotten until, stirred by my visit, the lyrics rose up inside my bones. For me, Israel was the trip of a lifetime, a true mountaintop experience.

Friends have asked me, "What was the highlight of the trip?" That was hard to answer, because I was like a child full of wonder during the entire journey. I couldn't twirl around fast enough in my attempt not to miss a thing. Certainly many moments stood out: from Masada, the mountain range that offered fascinating ancient history and watercolor views that drizzled into the Dead Sea; to the dear man in the midst of his life's closing chapter; to a friend's baptism in the Jordan River; to the perfectly tended Resurrection Garden; to the evening we visited the Wailing Wall. Oh, yes, and my visit to the Jerusalem Market. That, my friend, was a pinnacle experience . . .

Our vehicle arrived at the market along with twelve

other buses from our tour. The street seemed congested, but we weren't surprised, because we had heard the following day was Jerusalem Day, a celebration of the city being in Jewish possession. That meant it was a joyous day but also a day of caution, for, just in case you hadn't heard, not everyone in the Middle East is pleased the city is in Israel's hands.

En route, we had noticed Jerusalem flags hanging from porches and in windows. What we hadn't expected was the pedestrian hubbub in the market streets. Evidently schools had released their children in groups to browse the market, which added to the festivities and certainly to the congestion.

In Jerusalem, groups of children aren't allowed to move about unless they're escorted by armed guards; so one or two guards, sometimes mothers with rifles slung over their backs, traveled with the children. With so many school children present, the place was swarming with guards.

In addition, out-of-town visitors poured into the town and into the market by the busload. Many had come in caravans to join in the celebration. Add to that the usual large contingent of tourists and the hundreds of soldiers milling about. Now pour all those folks into the winding market labyrinth of narrow passageways. Oh, but wait, I've failed to mention the most disconcerting addition of all: the cars. The walkways could barely hold the people on foot as they meandered from shop to shop, much less the cars that inched single-file through the people, causing pedestrians to press up against ancient walls to allow the vehicles to pass.

A helicopter circled above, and more buses of armed soldiers moved into the area. You couldn't help but notice.

On observing all this activity, our guide decided we should leave the controlled chaos. We had barely arrived, so this came as a surprise. We were instructed to quickly make our way back to the buses. As we turned into a narrow, brick-covered passageway, a line of cabs muscled their way through. There really was no room for them and us, and that's when tempers flared. The cab drivers were yelling at us to get out of their way; some folks were yelling back that we should be allowed through. Eventually, the cab drivers and the pedestrians negotiated their separate ways through the pencil-thin street.

After anxiety-producing moments, we were out into open spaces and boarded a bus. We had to temporarily commandeer one of the other tour buses and even had to "borrow" someone else's bus driver. Before we pulled out, more buses with armed soldiers arrived, and the young, rifle-toting Israeli men and women positioned themselves every ten feet along the main road that led to the market.

The Mountaintop: At last

When we returned to the hotel, we discussed how we felt about the turmoil. Much to the surprise of my friends and myself, I loved it. I felt as if we were experiencing the real-life tensions of the people, and I found that exhilarating. Don't get me wrong; I didn't want anyone to be in peril. Instead, it was that many of the sights one sees in Jerusalem are traditional tourist locales. The marketplace and the palpable apprehension that day was the real deal.

It turned out all was safe. In fact, it would be a month after our return to the States before escalating danger broke out in Israel. Perhaps what we experienced was the rumblings of coming conflict. Regardless, I'm grateful to be safely home, but the memory of the market stays with me.

Scripture instructs us to pray for the peace of Jerusalem. That has taken on deeper meaning since my trip and since conflict has broken out. I wonder about the safety of people we met—storeowners, guides, hotel employees, and young children in the streets who waved greetings to us. Yes, mountaintop encounters offer us wider views of our world lest we stay narrow in our hearts' perspective and small in our prayers.

Old Testament Moses experienced a broadening of his perspective. But his expanded views weren't limited to the land and people; he also encountered God in new ways, which by Moses's accounts were both scary and glorious.

We can only imagine returning from a mountaintop with God's presence still resting upon us. This desert prophet's meeting with God was so illuminating that he was covered in glory light. Can you picture an incandescent man descending from a mountain? I've seen people brighten up with joy and happiness on occasion, but I've never seen anyone actually light up. Nonetheless, love does light up a landscape. My friend Lana was in flight to a conference when she was caught up in a soaring conversation. The young man in his late twenties seated beside her shared his story of meeting the woman of his dreams, a story that Lana in turn shared with me.

The young man, let's call him Will, was a successful businessman who was walking down a crowded street when the beauty of a young lady passing by caught his eye. Then something happened to Will that had never occurred before. He felt a sense of urgency that if he didn't turn around and go after that young woman, he would regret it the rest of his life. In an instant, Will caught up with her (we'll call her Abby), introduced himself, and asked if he could buy her coffee. Charmed by his smile and what she perceived to be his warm heart, Abby accepted. As the weeks and then months unfolded, so did their love for each other.

Will told Lana that he wanted to make his proposal to

Abby a pinnacle experience, and he really meant that. Get this: Will was, unbeknownst to Abby, flying her parents and his to Austria, where the two families would gather on the Matterhorn.

There Will would have very special plans in place. He had been carving mandolins since he was a child, and he had carved one for Abby as an engagement gift, which he would present to her on bended knee atop the mountain. Inside the instrument would be Abby's stunning ring. (Lana didn't see the ring but believed it was stunning because, honey, it cost a bundle.)

While all this was taking place on the mountaintop, Will had made arrangements to have Abby's hotel room filled with lilies, her favorite flower. When she returned, hopefully stunned and excited about the proposal, she would be greeted by the beauty and dancing fragrance of the flowers that represented Will's love.

How dreamy is that? As far as love stories go, I'd have to say that one rates high on my list of real-life romance. Yet when our Prince, our Lily of the Valley, leaves the heights of heaven to receive us as his bride, every other love story we know will pale in comparison. Even Will's.

Our Groom, who will surprise us one day with his return, will come in all his glory for his church. Then we shall see not just the reflection of his countenance on

others, but we shall see him for who he is—the Light of
the World.

Until that bright and glorious day, we are called to
occupy the valley. It will take determination, resolve, and
zeal to live well here. It will also require us to keep short
accounts with God and others. In other words, don't let
things build up inside of you. When things are unsettled,
they leave us the same way.

I write this at a time when I'm trying to wrestle free
from resentment and to forgive someone who has hurt me
deeply. I've learned that pride can bind us to bitterness,
and given time, bitterness will defile our motives and dis-
rupt our health. I'm reminded that forgiving another person doesn't make that individual right, but it will release
us from the foothold of the enemy and the acidic qualities
of resentment.

The valley isn't easy or fair. Justice comes later, after
Christ's return. We shouldn't expect ease and fairness to
permeate our existence until we hear the trump of God at
Christ's return.

I'm grateful that every once in a while we're invited to a
mountaintop experience that floods us anew with a chorus
of hope so we can maintain a wider perspective. Of course,
we need to be aware that even the trek to the top of a peak
holds treachery. I don't know of any climbers who reach

the pinnacle without paying a price. Bumps, bruises, cuts, broken bones, frostbite, sunburn, sprains. Yet somehow, once atop the mountain, the price seems to fade in light of the view's splendor.

Our valley-trekking, desert-crossing, mountain-climbing friend Moses made his last trip up a mountain to see the Promised Land. It was God's gift to a tired traveler. Moses, 120 years old, after seeing from that mount the land his people would occupy, died.

Here's the strange part about his death: his bones were never found.

This is my theory: I think they're still up there, and when no one is around, they rattle out and dance. Perhaps at night, under the moon, we might catch a glimpse of a solitary figure waltzing about with his staff. After all, Moses not only saw Earth's land of promise, but when he dropped his body suit along with his bones for heaven's glory, he saw home for the first time.

Until we leave this rugged valley called Earth, we should keep dancing. Dance until the trumpet sounds. Dance until the marriage feast is spread. Dance until you hear the Savior welcome you to the heights of home.